"Writing powerfully from the heart, Miller tells a compelling story of her family's surviving and even thriving in the wake of devastating events in the lives of their children. With humility, vulnerability, and warmth, she does not shy away from the pain of loss and betrayal but faces it all head-on with courage and leads us gently through the losses of abuse into hope. Love is costly and demands more than we think we can give, but the rewards are beyond measure. This family's story bears that out in so many life-giving ways. I appreciate her and her husband's willingness to let us in on her family's struggle and the courage it took to bring the truth to light, to allow those hurt to tell their story, and to do all in their power to protect from future harm. Every parent should read this book."

—The Rev. Dr. Heather Wright, author of *Redeeming Eve: Finding Hope Beyond the Struggles of Life* and *Small Group Leadership as Spiritual Direction*, and coauthor of *Sacred Stress: A Radically Different Approach to Using Life's Challenges for Positive Change*

"What a beautiful, thought-provoking, very powerful, heart-wrenching story. A story truly about true faith, love, and miracles. This is a story that needs to be written and read. I shudder at how many people are secretly living a version of this. Maybe this story can give them the help they need. It is a message that needs to get out there."

—Misty Smith, spiritual life coach

"The author has written a hauntingly beautiful account of a family torn apart by tragedy and rebuilt by strength, love, and faith. The story of trauma and the insidious ways that it affects people's lives and the ripple effect it has on the whole family is eloquently shared and leaves a mark of deep sadness yet deep faith in the power of human connection and healing. I am humbled by the strength of the author to persevere and to find the positives among the rubble. A must-read for anyone looking for a renewed sense of faith in the human spirit."

—Sandra Birch, licensed clinical social worker
and trauma specialist

"I have been an ordained priest for forty-six years. I have also been a practicing family therapist. After reading *Buried Saints*, I was struck by the depth of human pain that innocent young people have to endure and survive. There is no minimizing human suffering. Yet our capacity for resiliency is amazing. In the story of *Buried Saints*, the deeper underpinnings of faith have contributed to weaving threads of resiliency. It is, tragically, an all-too-familiar story in our society. Yet we are not without resources. Everyone can be inspired by this story of hope."

—Liam G. Collins, ordained priest

"Seldom have I come across a story that is equal parts purpose, principle and passion—where, within and throughout, the whole is greater than the sum of its parts. Kudos to Brin Miller for being one of the rare authors to accomplish that feat."

—Brian Goldthorpe, www.messagingmastered.com

BURIED
SAINTS

BURIED SAINTS

A MEMOIR

BRIN MILLER

SHE WRITES PRESS

Published 2019
Printed in the United States of America
ISBN: 978-1-63152-509-4 (pbk)
ISBN: 978-1-63152-510-0 (ebk)
Library of Congress Control Number: 2018958079

Book design by Stacey Aaronson

For information, address:
She Writes Press
1569 Solano Ave #546
Berkeley, CA 94707

She Writes Press is a division of SparkPoint Studio, LLC.

BURIED SAINTS

✍ PREFACE

WHEN I WAS A KID. TO TAKE A PHOTO YOU HAD TO SNAP the shot, finish the film roll, and wait for it to be processed by hand. It could take weeks to get back tangible evidence of that special event. You relived the day on paper weeks after the actual moment had passed.

Now, though, no more waiting—you can instantly review the moment on a screen just seconds after it happens. And you can instantly delete the imperfect shots like they *never* happened. The gratification of having captured the perfect shot or deleting something unseemly is a simple click away. Today, "Say cheese!" is instantaneously followed by "Mommy, let me see it."

Life looks neater and tidier without the moments before and after a perfect picture. The second when the wind blew your hair, covering your face just at the exact wrong time. Or your smile wasn't ready, so the picture actually caught a frown and a wrinkled chin. The awkwardness, even if it is funny, doesn't get showcased in an album or frame. The imperfect or embarrassing gets cut.

Growing up, I made promises to myself that I would never be the mom wearing pajamas at the bus stop or who went to nursery school drop-off with my hair standing on end, still in my slippers. Then one day life snuck up on me. A series of days that turned into months and years.

My story is filled with images of one eye open and half a smiling face. Messed-up hair and stained clothes. This is a picture of me screaming and of punch flying through the air just before it hits everything in its path. This is a picture of bloodred juice spraying the walls and the floor and the chairs simultaneously. This is a picture of the children, out on the street running from me, the mom gone crazy.

This is the story of how my family endured an incredible breach of trust, and my daughters endured unimaginable abuse. A story of how faith saved us all, but only after that Hawaiian Punch bled across the kitchen floor like my heart blown wide open. This is the most imperfect of love stories. It's a story that might have stayed in the shoebox at the back of the closet; but it won't because it's mine, and love wins, so it is told.

❧ CHAPTER ONE

DAWSON WAS DONE. HE DIDN'T WANT TO BE MARRIED TO me anymore. Our fights were prevailing and our fists were up in defense. Nothing was the same anymore. There was too much loss and regret. Too many things for us to blame each other for.

The dinner dishes were all tucked in the dishwasher; the evening ritual of laundry folding while the girls took baths was done. The night was winding down.

By the end of any given day, eight o'clock was when my body ached the most and my legs had nearly taken their last steps and were longing for sleep. I was worn down from a three-year-old, a four-year-old, and a twelve-year-old. Tonight I was emotionally drained as well; the blame had sucked the life out of me. The kids had heard fight after fight—night after night. We never talked about it, but they knew the drill. Yelling, slamming, stomping, mommy crying, and daddy screaming. Each night its own scene in a horror film about parenting mistakes done to a tee.

Tonight, though, we had to go out to a cocktail party, putting a damper on our usual angry routine. I mustered up my standard game face and plastic smile, performing our *other* perfected routine.

It was okay. My face looked distressed even in my most relaxed moments. I have always been a reserved person. I don't trust people easily and for that I was used to being judged by my outward appearance, even on my best days. So the bad days like today—with my blank stare, the lump in my throat, and sore, puffy, dry eyes—wouldn't change anyone's first impression. No one ever bothered asking me if I was all right. It was easier to assume my life was perfect and I was your typical type-A unapproachable snob. Blond hair, blue eyes, always dressed nicely with the tall, dark, handsome, perfect-looking husband, and kids that followed suit. I'm sure there were some people who envied my picture of perfection.

The babysitters came, so I put energy into my steps. We had two babysitters. There was no particular reason except they were best friends and I was close with both of their mothers and had been for a long time. Since they were only twelve going on thirteen, it never seemed like overkill to me. Actually, I liked it. It made me feel like my girls were safe. I had known both sitters since they were about eight months old themselves. It was more like family than a service. All the same, to save my pride, I avoided their eyes as I gave them directions for the rest of the night. Our girls, Kennedy and Taylor, would go down for bed after a small bit of TV. When the school fundraiser was over, Dawson would drop me back home and take the sitters home on his way to go pick up Tom, my stepson, when his swim practice was over. I would return around nine. Still ducking my head and acting busy, I walked toward the door. My defeated body marched mindlessly outside and to the car. Dawson was waiting in angry protest, having already escaped the house to avoid the sitters and me. He didn't look at me, only straight ahead at the road, hands gripping the wheel. I was turned toward the passenger-side window anyway. Silence chilled the air. It was a short drive, and there really was nothing to say.

I HAVE FIVE to seven long, deep wrinkles on my forehead and unmemorable eyes. I don't have a soft inviting look when I'm distracted or afraid. I'm the kind of person who looks judgmental and like someone to be afraid of.

My expressions have always plagued me. Worse, my expressions have always robbed me of looking sensitive. Because of this I have always carried a voice in my head that wished for someone to notice who I am on the inside instead of trusting their perceptions of how I appear outwardly. Just this little voice that screams, "Ask me if I'm okay and be there when I answer no." I have heard this voice all my life.

All the same, I wouldn't wait long for anyone to ask tonight. We walked into the open door of the party. As usual the main cluster of school parents was in the kitchen. Following the noise, we walked through the house to join the crowd. Dawson went left and I went right. I tried to put on a smile as I set the appetizer I was asked to bring on the table. Chatting about nothing seemed to absorb enough time to make the party pass. It was a kindergarten fundraiser, so almost every face was new. Though I was trying not to be self-conscious, I couldn't help but imagine that my face looked frozen and expressionless, like I had just completed Botox treatments earlier that day. Dawson was across the room introducing himself to the other dads. I could hear his voice booming across the kitchen. He was easygoing and often the life of the party. He had a knack for being able to compartmentalize fights and shut down his bad mood when needed.

Hours later Dawson circled back to the door, signaling to me that it was time to go. As I heard him and distracted myself by pretending to get some food, the weight of the world just felt like it was about to swallow me whole. It seemed like midnight when we finally left, but it was right around 8:45 p.m., just as planned. I wrapped up my conversation and left robotically. I felt defeated after putting up a front for the public. It seemed useless to meet elementary school parents now, since after the divorce, the girls and I could very well be living with my mother. Though nothing had been decided, the loud arguments with the even louder threats shook me enough to imagine all the what-ifs of a divorce tragedy. So it was easy for me to wonder if my kids would even be in this school come a month from now.

In the haze that again consumed me on the short drive, Dawson dropped me at home and picked up the babysitters to take them home. I walked into the house to a moment of silence. It felt heavenly. Even a little bit light. I took a few deep breaths and attempted to enjoy this moment, but then my fear of a second divorce turned to anger, and I decided to take my ten minutes of solitude to vent to a friend. Claire had been my neighbor during my first marriage. Also divorced, she and I had remained close. She was the mother of one of my sitters, so I knew she was up waiting for her daughter to come home.

Once Dawson returned home, I quickly hung up the phone. He hastily entered the house, stomped upstairs, banged around, and slammed doors open and closed. He wanted to finish the argument that we had put on hold to go out. He never wanted to do that by talking; he just stomped upstairs, banged around items, and slammed doors open and closed. I was standing in the bedroom when he came in. The cathedral ceiling echoed all his noises. Though most nights this room was a warm and comforting place of rest, there were nights that were far from peaceful. The nights when he reached for his red-and-black gym bag. Tonight was one of those nights. Angrily packing it with two days' worth of clothes, Dawson still managed to keep them folded and wrinkle-free at the same time. Once the bag was piled high, he hastily grabbed things in the bathroom and stuffed his brown dopp kit on top. All the running around and packing was loud and frantic. "This is it!" he exclaimed. He was moving out. All I could do was focus on how that stupid dopp kit would fall out the top of the bag if he stomped out.

For now, moving out meant he was storming down the hall to "Daddy's sick bedroom" until he could find some extra money. This was his final straw. He was miserable, and he wanted a divorce.

It wasn't the first time he had wanted a divorce. Yet each time he declared it, I felt as if a vise had just taken its last and tightest turn on my chest. This time I couldn't think about it. Word after word coming at me made my body tremble. "I'm done. I'm calling a lawyer tomorrow. I don't want to talk to you. This is it. I really mean it this time. I need to spend more time on myself. I need to focus on work. I can't live with you anymore. Your control has gone too far." Yes, I had heard it before, but this time . . . this time something was bubbling higher in his anger than normal. This time it was more intense than any of our arguments about kids or alcohol. It was different. It was true something felt deeply wrong, but I didn't think it was the usual money or Tom arguments. It wasn't just my general distrust of people or Dawson's anger. As deeply as I tried, I just couldn't name it.

After he stormed down the hallway, my focus shifted to

the blue walls that were spinning around me. Maybe my head was spinning and the blue was still. *I hate that sports bag. It doesn't even fit all his stuff. How the heck does he not have wrinkled clothes? I hate ironed clothes. I hate his ironed clothes.*

What will we do? I thought frantically. *Where will I go? How will I make money again? Will I really stoop to living with my mother? Oh my mother, she will love this. Oh, she will fix me! How will I trust again? Will I hate him? Will we hate each other? What will happen to Tom? What will happen to me? And my dad? I married my dad? Maybe I married his dad. Worse, maybe I married his mother.*

In our house the drama and the catastrophe were mounting. My brain felt ready to explode.

MEANWHILE, TUCKED IN their brand-new big-girl beds, Kennedy at four and Taylor at three talked to each other about silly things to keep from hearing the fighting. I had thought they were asleep, but lately they seemed to talk a lot more before they closed their eyes. They had each other. I supposed they just needed sister time before they settled in each night. No noise came from Tom's room. He was alone.

Still in disbelief in my room and mentally floating in and out between pain and anger, I stressed about what would happen to Tom. That thought could consume me even more than worries of my own daughters. I knew the girls and I would be okay, but what about Tom? He wouldn't have me anymore. I was sure I was his only hope. His dad was consumed with himself—and his mother, well, she was just a trainwreck. I kept Tom's life on schedule and on track. I was the one he leaned on when he needed help. I was the one he called first for homework, sports, friends, and advice.

My mind raced. I felt crippled lying on my bed. I cried. My body tensed. Rosacea covered my face with its heat and redness, and my eyes drooped from fatigue. After a few moments I was just numb, a dull ache inside my head, with eyes that felt dry when they blinked; tension coursed through my neck and shoulders, muscles eager to breathe but afraid to loosen up enough for oxygen.

I was instantly jolted back into the present moment with Dawson's yell from down the hallway: "I want a divorce," he repeated. "I'm done."

After his last threat, my energy was completely depleted. My head was frozen, and my body could not move. Numbness was not a resolution but a temporary solution that helped me slow the trembling. I worked my brain hard to achieve numbness. It tamed the anger and helped me survive one critical moment at a time.

Finally, I broke my silence: "Fine, move down the hall. Take aalllll the time you want. I'm not discussing a divorce. I don't care what you do, but I'm not discussing a divorce!" It was useless, though—he had already moved down the hall with or without my permission.

There is no doubt my head was swirling with what a divorce would actually look like, but in reality divorce just didn't seem like the option to me. It didn't add up. My heart declared it wasn't the end. There was pain in my chest just thinking about it. I didn't have answers that weren't filled with blame and venom. I didn't know how to talk unless I was also pointing the finger, but I wouldn't discuss divorce. He could have all the time he needed with his stupid bag and his "sick room," but a divorce wasn't in the cards.

I was once told the body owns the score. It was a medical reference to trauma. The body remembers more than the mind. Regardless of how miserable we were, my heart and my body weren't ready to let go. It's unexplainable; he was right. Nothing had really been the same these days. We could say it was the death of Morgan, our dog, but these weren't feelings of mourning. The house did seem vacant without her tail hitting the floor. No shuffling as she rolled over—all eighty-five hairy, loving, black-and-brown pounds—when I spoke thoughts out loud. I desperately felt the void of her unconditional love and approval. Truth is, we were all off-kilter, having buried her only two weeks ago. But at the core, our issues weren't the dog. The truth was, over a short period we had built up a lot of anger toward each other. Our young love had been short-lived and we had had problems right from the start.

✑ CHAPTER TWO

NOTHING IN YOUR LIFE REALLY PREPARES YOU FOR MARRIAGE the way you end up experiencing it. It's true that how you grow up sheds light on your potential actions or behaviors. But in the merging of two separate backgrounds, a marriage is very rarely the same as it was for one's parents. I was not prepared for the compromise. It never occurred to me that I would have to mold my ways around someone else's.

I had practically everything I wanted growing up. We lived in a traditional colonial house. We had two cars until we needed three—then we had three. I never longed for anything. I was hardly into the world of name-brand things, but when I was, I just saved my money to get them. I was pretty simple, and I was okay with that.

All my primary school years were pretty routine. Wake up, get ready for school, pick out clothes, brush teeth, go to the bathroom.

After school—thirty minutes of TV. There was only one TV set, so whoever got off the bus and inside the family room first got to choose the show. We spent many a half hour watching Bob Ross on the *Joy of Painting*. I didn't get to the TV first very often.

Then we would load up the car to head to swimming. Two hours of swimming every day except Sunday. I just went with the flow every day, rarely asking questions or voicing discontentment.

After practice I would head to the shower. Sometimes to break up the monotony, my friends and I would mix it up a bit: boys would shower in the girls' locker room, girls would shower in the boys'. In general, I was too busy to be in trouble.

Get dressed, blow-dry hair, and finally the locker room door opened and a loud bellow rang out: "The car is leaving!!" Once home, slurp down an overcooked, tasteless dinner with milk, do homework, and go to bed. Rise and repeat.

DAD WENT TO work, went to the bar, and came home somewhere in the middle of dinner and homework. Mom taught during the day and took care of the four of us before and after her work hours. My parents rarely hugged, never held hands, and certainly didn't kiss. They just *were*.

My parents lived a married life from different histories. My mom's parents worked hard and served their country. They saved and planned for future what-ifs. My grandparents on my mother's side were typical Depression-era keepers and set an exceptional example of satisfaction in simplicity. They split one beer every night. They had vintage 1970s furniture, not for style but because they didn't need to replace what still worked. They even got an 800 number for all their grand-children to call them on so no one would have to use their own money—but then only talked for a set limit of time because back then each minute was really expensive. They were close role models in our lives, and I saw fit to follow in many of their ways. I saved my money and didn't take big risks.

My dad's family inherited buckets of money and worked enough to play. He and his seven siblings argued a lot and lived in constant discord with one another. My dad had his first trust fund at thirty and felt compelled when money got tight to remind us it was *his* money.

But even trust fund money runs short, and Dad still needed to work to support four kids, a house, and a wife. So as jobs became scarce locally, the interviews moved him farther and farther from home, thus he traveled a lot during my middle and high school years for "work." In between trips were many nights I spent putting Dad to bed. The square bottle filled with butterscotch-colored liquid would sit on the stone table next to Dad's TV chair at 5:00 p.m. When there were no "interviews" and there weren't any "projects," his days were spent on the computer and ended with his nights in front of the TV. As the scotch, Glenlivet to be exact, disappeared inch by inch, the TV volume would increase bit by bit. Each night the bottle would appear and so also came the clinking of the ice cubes into the glass and the sound of his sips. When he drank, I couldn't focus on anything else. How long could I sit there in front of the only TV in our house before an exit was acceptable? Time slowed with each passing second. Anxiety rose with each clink and sip. He never exploded on us in a drunken rage, but the discomfort of that possibility was always there.

My parents lived parallel lives that rarely crossed until my parents' marriage ended; then it was an intersection of chaos. After thirty years together, things spontaneously exploded and burned every existing childhood memory I had, both good and bad. At twenty-four, getting ready for my wedding to Kerry—my first husband—I came home one day to find my petite mother, at five feet two, rolling a six-foot professional work desk down the stairs and out the front door.

She smiled when I got to the door and said, "Can you help?" as if this was like pulling out the crockpot or weeding the garden.

I have two older brothers and a younger sister. I was the most naïve of my siblings. I didn't seek out anything that wasn't in front of me. I thought my mother and father were perfect and that our little world was all I needed. Worse, I thought we were normal.

Sure, Dad's lost jobs were replaced with drinking, traveling for "interviews," and consulting leads, which turned into lengthy spells living in different states. Whatever the real reason he was gone, my parents always called it work, but mostly it was just unpaid projects that never actually led to any money. Yet there I was one afternoon, helping move this enormous desk filled with my dad's paperwork out the front door and onto the front lawn.

My mom was always there for us when we were kids, but she had a controlling side to her that overcompensated for my dad's loss of control. Often, to counter his drunken example, my mom would lecture: "One in four people become alcoholics. One in four," she warned ominously. There were four of us, of course. And Mom was sure one of us couldn't escape this predestined fate. In her mind, one of us would surely repeat the days of rising out of the bed only to put on a pretend happy face, determined to survive the day in order to get to the first evening drink. This terrifying vision of my future wore on me like a heavy cape weighing me down and reminding me of the nights Dad used to be glued to the TV at its highest volume, while Mom was upstairs in her room closed off to the rest of the world. It was a lonely, sad projection of our lives, and it drove me to work any way I could to avoid becoming the "one."

❧

YET JUST WHEN the tension became too much to endure, relief would come when Dad would convince Mom and himself he wasn't an alcoholic. 7Up by the case would pack the refrigerator, and the clink of ice would be replaced with a refreshing whoosh and fizz once the soda can was opened. And a crush and clank as it ultimately landed crinkled in the blue recycling bin. In his backward way of thinking, eight cans of 7Up a day proved he wasn't addicted to alcohol. Confirming it as a temporary fix, though, the 7Up would eventually disappear and inevitably the ice cubes returned to replace the whoosh and the crushing of a can. The TV volume would be back on high, and the discomfort inside me would rise again.

When I was in the midst of it, I didn't realize these things weren't normal. It wasn't until I left home and began to discover life for myself that I realized my upbringing was dysfunctional. It was my marriage to Kerry that first revealed how one-sided my childhood had taught me to be. It was really easy for me to completely ignore his needs. My go-to behaviors and reactions weren't workable at all in a relationship; they were really just survival tactics for me.

๛ *CHAPTER THREE*

MY FIRST MARRIAGE ENDED AT THE AGE OF TWENTY-eight after four years. Kerry and I had grown up together as high school sweethearts, but we didn't know how to be grown-ups together. True, when he went off to college, we had broken up and dated other people, but we eventually made our way back to talking and then seeing each other.

I graduated college at twenty-two and started floundering the day after graduation. I lived my life with a clear plan up until the day I had a degree, but then had no idea what to do with myself. So while I was lacking anything else to do, I drove out west to Wyoming with my brother, who had been hoping I would say no when, out of pity, he asked me to come with him. We passed the time without any real direction. He was taking a much-needed break after graduate school, and I was lost and unsure about my future. After six months I longed to be home by the water instead of up in the mountains. Upon returning home, Kerry and I started seeing each other more frequently again and easily fell right back into the familiar comfort of our high school days. And before anyone could even notice, we were quite quickly engaged. While my parents were in the middle of a raging divorce, I married, and within the next year settled into our new house in the suburbs—all by the age of twenty-five.

SADLY. THOUGH. THAT marriage was a scaled-down version of my childhood. In general our new life together was a familiar and easy routine. Sure we had a bit of a social life, but it wasn't deep. It was more for show and it passed the time. But after a couple of years, serenity started to erode, as we never really moved our friendship into something deeper and more mature. We were becoming parallel. I could see it, and I was terrified of it.

Stalled, I wasn't prepared for change and dug my heels in. Slowly but surely our lives drifted into increasingly frequent disagreements, nights of anxiety, and heavy anticipation of an ending. Still young, we quite easily split. And just like that, we said our good-byes and went our separate ways. One trip to court, a faxed divorce decree, and a pleasant sale of the house. No drama or fuss or complication. Since we had never really intertwined, it was easy to go our separate ways, continuing down our own unique paths.

I HAD GROWN up in a full house. There were always people around. I had roommates at every step of life before marriage. I had only even had my own room for a short time before Kerry and I were married. Divorced, I was alone, completely alone. Without the house or dog, I was now renting a small apartment a town away. Not even my neighbors were familiar.

Alone, I was both at peace and yet completely terrified with the unfamiliar feelings and thoughts I was now able to experience within myself. It was wonderful and awful. Before my divorce, any alone time was quickly filled with company. I had never truly experienced what it was like to be on my own for any length of time and certainly not what it was like to be lonely.

I worked hard and continued up the corporate ladder to fill my emptiness. My friends were planning babies and baptisms, even first birthdays. I was dating and entertaining clients. I had more in common with my friends' husbands than my friends and no swimming pool or swimming team to retreat to. I felt my awkwardness absorbing me.

Believing wholeheartedly I was never meant to actually live alone, I was open to every blind date anyone wanted to set me up on. Since I had grown up always having a boyfriend, I had no experience with dating. I embraced the distraction and adventure.

Everyone had someone special for me and soon one Bob was the same as the next. Over time I developed a nickname system for each of them. Dating filled my boredom. In the beginning it kept my loneliness at bay and it filled my mind with purpose. So my mantra became "Yes, I'll go," no matter the who, what, or where.

There was Match.com. It gave me seven matches to the perfect man. I emailed one of them. Of course I said yes for coffee at my favorite spot and a walk around the beach. He offered me his number . . . but he was not a match.

But it didn't take long before the fun of dating wore thin. I became frustrated and a bit choosy. If they were arrogant, I didn't want them. If they were late or had bad table manners, I didn't waste my time with long encounters. I was not going to fix anyone. Life was meant to be exciting, and I was going to keep it that way. One day I would wake up and someone was going to have fit in.

The nicknames made it all the more fun. Everyone had someone they knew who they were certain would be my perfect match. There was "Mark Spitz," full, dark-brown head of hair, bushy eyebrows, and a mustache. He showed up forty-five minutes late. Automatic no!

"Drunk Dial": He had the dialing problem, not me! He had three glasses of wine on the table at any given point in the dinner. He kindly offered to help with my sex life if I didn't have one.

My chiropractor, appropriately named the "Inappropriate Chiropractor" because he wanted to take me out, or so he said one day while I was half-dressed on a table and he was cracking my back. He assured me I would not be ruining his marriage since it was "already dead." As I walked out of my appointment, I was sure to say good-bye to the receptionist—or should I say *his wife*!?

"Not-Sure-If-He-Is-Married Man," turned out he was indeed married.

"Coach.com" (nicknamed after his place of business): We met out at a bar. He was tall and skinny. Well dressed and decent looking. About twenty minutes into talking and with half a drink left, he went to the bathroom. Then he returned and hurriedly flagged down the waiter. Apparently he *forgot* he had dinner plans and had to go. His car service was already right out in front of the hotel.

"Runner Boy" and I went to a tapas restaurant. As we were looking at the menu, designed for family-style eating, he revealed that he had a sharing problem. In fact, he said, he had an eating disorder. He could not stop eating things once he started. Even his hypnosis didn't completely work to solve it. I ran.

The men went from bad to worse, but I persevered and dated more. "Rugby Guy," "Baby," "Bob the Bore," "Shorty"— each one worse than the next.

Until "Snaggletooth." We met at Bed, a hip new NYC restaurant. It had beds and drinks but no food!

He was on time but short with bad teeth—hence the nickname, Snaggletooth. They were not even yellow but some shade of orange—I assumed smoker's teeth.

In the end, we shared a cab to the train station and said good-bye. No need for a polite "I'll call you." Nothing.

One disaster of a man after another ultimately left me exasperated. I was defeated. I surrendered!

And then I met "Bar Guy." He was a two-for-one.

IT WAS THAT chance encounter that finally ended my floundering ways one evening. I could feel his words going right through me like knives. I had just completed one last blind date too many the night before. I was out to have fun, not listen to this guy complaining about his ex-wife. So I leaned in and asserted myself.

"Are you from here? Is your ex-wife from here?" I asked.

To both questions he answered, "No."

"Well, I am from here and so is my ex-husband, so you have no idea what it is like to be talked about in town."

And that was it. I had thrown my bitterness out there, and he still wanted my business card.

It was just after midnight on a Thursday. The friend whom I'd shown up with was drunk and I was sober, waiting to drive her home. I was sour; dating sucked and men were stupid. I was exhausted by the whole scene. On the way out the door, though, I felt a set of hands grasp my elbows. It was Dawson, Mr. Tall, Dark, and Secretly Hoping He Was Available. He spun me around and asked where I was going.

"Home!" I retorted.

Annoyed now, I turned to leave. As I did, he caught my lips with his. His lips applied a confident amount of pressure to seal his intent and just as abruptly he released me. Without a second's hesitation I finished my turn and left. Out the door and out of sight, though, my knees buckled. I giggled, but then reality quickly struck—I didn't believe in magic. I was going home.

CHAPTER FOUR

I FEEL FORTUNATE TO HAVE HAD MY FIRST TRUE LOVE
at fifteen. Though it taught me a lot, it did not last. So when
I met Dawson, I was openhearted and ready for commitment
and family, but I was more protective of myself. I wasn't going
to spend time trying to fix anyone. I thought I was prepared
to right the mistakes of my past and start again. I now knew
better about what went wrong in my relationships. With
Dawson I was reduced to high school butterflies and eagerly
awaiting calls all over again. Overcome by this familiar feeling,
I convinced myself the new me could triumph over anything.
In my excitement I was willing to overlook complications and
bumps in the road, as long as I didn't have to give the issues
time or attention.

I issued a pass for Dawson's four-year-old son, Tom, from
his first marriage. They came as a package deal. It seemed
only natural to me that a father and a son would be a team;
unlike what you often hear about, where a dad disappears in
divorce and only shows up every other weekend. They often
rode bikes on the weekends. They traveled together. They
skied together. They were close, as he told it—so of course
that's what I chose to believe.

Tom came with Dawson and a bag of groceries to make
dinner for our second date. He was a quiet and sad little boy.
White-blond hair and piercing blue eyes greeted me when he

was able to look upward. His face often missed a smile. His chin drooped and his baby blues were often blank. He was a little lost that first meeting. His favorite truck had been left behind, and he was anxious without it by his side. While Dawson raced home to grab the truck and relieve Tom's anxiety, Tom and I had twenty minutes to ourselves. In spite of his initial shyness and hesitance, he somehow managed to reach out for a simple handhold and a loving touch. In fact, right from the start he sought basic emotional acts from me that typically a mother would give. It wasn't too long into our courtship that I learned his mother had no affection to offer.

I was the new girlfriend who came along just before his parents' long, argumentative divorce was final. Sara, Dawson's soon-to-be ex-wife, had been told she couldn't have children, so they were both surprised by her pregnancy with Tom. That temporarily halted the divorce proceedings, but in the end, they just couldn't live together. I was thirteen years younger than Sara and to my knowledge could complete the family filled with children and activities that Dawson wanted. To her, I was most definitely the enemy, and she was going to make that fact known. Before me, Tom's parents had fought, and now I was making it worse.

Through all my mother's problems with my dad, she was rock stable. So it was only natural that I thought Sara should be too; after all she was a mother. When Dawson and I met, he saw Tom two or three days a week. By then I had purchased a small house back in my hometown. As our relationship grew stronger, Dawson began staying with me. Three months after we met, he moved in. The nights with Tom didn't change—they were just at my house. Despite Sara's anger at Dawson for introducing Tom to "another woman," she found increasingly disruptive ways to contact Dawson for parenting advice. Her calls and confrontations became upsetting, most especially to Tom. Every step of the way, there were complications when it came to Sara. She loved to confront me at the school pickup line when I was getting Tom while Dawson was at work. She confronted us both on the baseball field where Dawson and I would just be watching the game. Sara was constantly in my face. She was angry, and I was the target.

Simultaneously my relationship with Dawson continued to intensify. We had dinners and drinks. We met each other's friends. Right from the start I could tell that Dawson was the outward, social, life-of-the-party guy. He was the first to liven up the room and the last to go home at the end of the night. He could certainly work a crowd. I'd never before dated the life of the party. I couldn't keep up with the drinking most nights, and it often felt like he had a hollow leg to absorb the excess alcohol. This was all new to me, but as intimidated as I was, I wanted to keep up.

It was an innocent young love, naïve and irresponsible, yet bore a heaviness about it. Individual moments could be shielded, but the big picture forced itself on us often. Dawson's friends subtly voiced not liking me, and Sara maintained her conviction that I was not to be around "her son." Condemnation from our family and friends was constant.

We heeded no warnings. After we met in May, we moved in with each other by July. From the outset, life in our house was predictable and choreographed just as it had been when I was a child. Breakfast was always before school, and we left for the drive to school every morning at eight thirty. Pickup was exactly at three—Dawson and Tom or Tom and I, whatever the combination. The closer Dawson and I became, the more interwoven the routine became. We arrived on time for everything and we were always prepared. Dinner was always at five and bedtime was always seven thirty. These were qualities of raising kids that Dawson and I strongly shared, and they seemed to work, especially for Tom.

Sure, we had our issues. We grappled with relationship compromises and with issues in raising Tom. He had been hurt, he had trouble in school, he had social fears, but most concerning of all to me—he was petrified of the water. The first time I heard the bellowing, "Dad! Dad save me!!" it stopped me cold. He could and *did* drive any pool party crowd into dead silence. The sound of his fear gave every parent a moment of panic. Was it *my* child who was about to fall under? In a deeply heartfelt way I related to Tom's fears. His anxiety on the whole made sense to me, but his fear of water needed to be changed.

I was the outsider in Dawson's world. The new girl who had captured the heart of the eligible bachelor that every woman, married or not, wanted. He was the life of the party. He was six feet two and often mistaken for Rob Lowe or Charlie Sheen, depending on whether you liked good boys or bad. He was smart and funny and looked like the complete and perfect package.

I heard the whispers as I walked by: "Who is that plain Jane?" and "How did *she* end up with him?" Followed by statements like, "It won't last." Going out felt like an adult version of the movie *Mean Girls*. They targeted me in a relentless effort to make me feel uncomfortable or to remind me that I didn't fit in. The tests against me were endless and always insidious enough to have Dawson wondering if it was all just a figment of my imagination. After all, his inner circle would *never* try to hurt him. My anxiety naturally brewed over time and led to arguments that pitted us against each other.

Yet soon we would circle back around and reengage in our young love. My defensiveness and hurt feelings would pass, and Dawson's apprehension would be restrained. We would focus again on our commitment to each other and focus less on the judgment that was being thrust upon us.

Dawson and I worked best when we had something to focus on. Often we really did believe in the same solutions, even if we took different paths to get to them. Tom, too, was a part of the team, and he would often start to work toward solutions for himself, like the moment he ventured to calm his fear of water with one simple question: "Brin, will you teach me how to swim? Like you did?"

Eventually, friends dialed back their judgment. Sara's dysfunction began to become predictable, which was oddly comforting. So in seven short months we had overcome the odds and were engaged. Now even the worst critics couldn't deny that I was here to stay. For better or for worse.

MY MOTHER CLAIMED I had become a swimmer because my brothers were and I wanted to follow them. I think I swam because there is no "awkward" in swimming. You can't be too tall or trip over your feet. Swimming leveled the playing field and smoothed out my self-doubt during my maturing years. Swimmers fit into their own society, and I rejoiced in that.

Swimming as a kid was the perfect routine to counterbalance the tension between my parents. In the pool I never had the questions I had on land. In the pool, the world was my oyster. Life was easy. Pace your speed, swim smart not hard. Be precise with your hands, don't forget the legs, use your stomach, and win. It always felt like the water was smooth and I was gliding over the top of it. Of course there were the rare days when my body felt like lead and every stroke felt like I was carving ice with my hands, but in general, I felt absolved of worry when I was in the pool.

I started swimming at the age of eight and finished at twenty-three. There was a certain kind of connectedness in the pool for me. It was the only time my mind and body were in sync. I was completely satisfied at the end of my college career. It had not always been easy, but I knew how to be counted on in the pool. "Some swimmers swim the same speed no matter the circumstances. You—you adjust. No matter what happens, you will adjust," my coach would say. And it was true. Adjusting was something I knew how to do.

I BELIEVE MY exact response to Tom asking me to teach him to swim was, "Oh sweetie!" with a bit of excitement and surprise. I jumped on the chance to help him solve his issue.

Dawson and I had been married a year and a half by now. In that time we had also moved into a new house. Tom was seven and I was newly pregnant. Dawson hadn't liked living in "my" house, so we'd sold it and moved into "our" house. It was a small fixer-upper, and we liked working on it together. In fact, when he and I were focused on a goal, we were unstoppable together. The projects kept us bonded. But

Dawson had been in and out of work and getting swim lessons for Tom took some planning. We weren't able to afford a pool club, and even a YMCA membership was a consideration. So he asked the only friend he had with a pool in the backyard if we could use it. That wasn't an easy request either. Though his friends tolerated me now, they made sure I knew they disapproved of the way I was parenting Tom. The favor was for Dawson, and I knew that. All the same, twice a week I would pick Tom up at summer camp and drive him twenty minutes away to a neighboring town where we would practice. By this time I was five months pregnant with Kennedy and growing rounder by the day. Once I was wet, though, the awkwardness of the environment and the multitude of unwanted feelings melted away, and I would always feel lighter both mentally and physically.

I played coach, and with time Tom learned to go back and forth in the fifteen-yard backyard pool. "Long arms, breathe to the side. Head down. Use your legs—they have the strongest muscles in your body," I would endlessly repeat. And by the end of the summer, he had a skill to showcase. Quite logically, that fall he joined our town's swim program.

My alone time with Tom was natural to me. I always felt that parenthood would come easily. Still without my own child, Tom gave me an opportunity to practice the nurturing qualities I longed to share. Having Tom in my life gave me peace in my soul where the feelings of failure from my previous marriage were hidden by my admittedly tough exterior.

By the time Tom conquered his fear of the water and was on the swim team, a new school year started, and our family added one more. Life was more of a roller coaster now; I was managing a new business after leaving my job in

New York City, our finances were not stable, our friendships were erratic, we were caring for a stepchild who now stayed four out of seven nights each week, and we added an infant to the mix. It quickly took a toll. We weren't dealing with the new-baby frenzy as much as we were enduring what seemed like endless discord. Sara was still confrontational, Dawson and I were drifting apart with drinking and distrust in between us, and sleepless nights were catching up to me.

Nonetheless Kennedy was a settling and welcome addition in my life. Admittedly her companionship filled a loneliness in me that was different than what Tom filled and that I didn't even know had been slowly growing within me. My pregnancy with her was extremely easy and we had a deep connection right from conception. I felt complete with this little poolside partner sitting comfortably next to me in her bucket carseat. She was small but chubby. She sat contentedly while passersby remarked on her rolls. She smiled endlessly for her brother.

Day after day I tried hard to believe that I had two children. I wanted to believe that we were one family, but inside I was conflicted. Having Kennedy engendered my parenting spirit more deeply, differently, than Tom had.

From the outside, Dawson and I looked like the perfect couple. We were almost always composed, social, and both working hard to maintain a steady family life. Soon after I decided to stay home, Dawson began commuting instead of me, and my new job was a work-from-home arrangement. He finally landed a stable job in New York City. On the inside, however, the pressure of Tom's competing lives and his two different households weighed heavily on everyone. Having our own baby certainly added tension. Finances, a new puppy, and a dawning realization of the unstable foundation of our relationship were all eroding our happiness. Arguing killed our naïve love; Dawson's "life of the party" drinking killed the romance. Life was becoming overwhelming. On top of it all were the nights I was alone while he was at business events, or just the nights where I fatigued of the excessive drinking and went home by myself—those were the most isolating of them all. I had so much fear being at home alone with all the lives I was responsible for, and I wondered if my childhood had set me up to fail again, not knowing how to handle my situation.

At thirty-three and with a dog, a stepchild, and a toddler, I had become my mother when Dawson actually *was* home, retreating to my room while the glass was emptied inch by inch downstairs. This time it was vodka, not scotch.

CHAPTER FIVE

WHENEVER DAWSON AND I WOULD FIGHT, HE ALWAYS threatened a divorce. It was the one thing that unhinged my internal security and brought me straight to the inner "little girl" who had been emotionally abandoned by her father and who craved love but felt a massive void. It was a threat that hurt, no matter how often it came and how little it was executed.

Entering into my relationship with Dawson, I thought I had all the answers, having been divorced before. I was strong on the outside and I thought my strength would overcome anything. It didn't serve me well though with kids, a house, and pets. Those were conditions that changed marriage in ways I had not anticipated and was not prepared to handle.

So I knew he had been "done" with our relationship before. He was most definitely done right after Kennedy was born, hence the late-night "work" events. I was done then too. I had actually planned an intervention for the drinking, but the DWI put a halt to that plan. Kennedy was all of six months old when he quit drinking for good. Yet he never followed through on being done with me and our marriage; he was just finished with drinking.

Getting sober in reality involves so much more than stopping drinking. Once you stop, you find that all the anger and resentment you once masked with alcohol are still there; you just have no way to hide them. And the triggers, well the whole family has them by the time a drunk stops drinking. It's like a house full of jumping beans and there's no way to contain all the movements. You are just all supposed to stop blaming and stop being mad, but the damage has already been done, and it blinds you too much to see your own personality anymore. You are no longer your own person; you are a collage of disappointments and letdowns.

As jumpy as I was most days, I also felt like I was living in an old spider's web with the left-behind shells of bodies, fractions of blown leaves, and particles of dirt that are still there because the spider had moved on. I felt like I needed to dust off all the children and my own hurt feelings that had been left behind. I felt like I needed to make myself look the part of the "perfect" family and pretend that the outward image was also true on the inside. I felt like I didn't know who my husband was as he overcame his challenges, and I felt like I didn't know who I was beyond my anger. Getting sober is sobering. It's a whole family's burden, and it takes time. Time you are tired of giving.

THE JOURNEY INTO sobriety was hard, but I had baby Kennedy. She gave me the strength I didn't have. She reminded me to dig deep. She was short and plump, just the way our doctor liked babies, two wrists and two ankles on each side. People would say, "I can see she likes to eat." She fit into my arms like an elbow noodle, so that is what we called her. I was busy with starting a new company, and she was always at my side. I was never alone. And she gave me strength and purpose. As I found myself feeling sad and low most days, Kennedy was a reason I needed to pick myself up, work harder, and adjust.

Months passed and she was my sounding board. We would sit, and I would talk and pretend that she was intently listening while we muddled through together, mom and baby. When she did finally start talking, her first words were strings, "Good job!" or "Let's go." It seemed like right from the beginning she communicated with definitive meaning. And I needed the positive outlook.

It soon became common practice for her to cheer on her father at times, such as while he was mowing the lawn. He also needed the positive encouragement. Sitting on the front step or walking alongside with her plastic kid mower, she would say, "Great job, Daddy. Go, go, go." It never got old.

KENNEDY'S YOUNG FACE was soft. Her freckles were perfectly balanced to the right and left of her nose. They looked like props placed there by a makeup artist. Her hair color was literally the perfect amount of dirty and blond. Hair colorists oohed and aahed when she would get a haircut. Strangers in seats next to her remarked on it, asking if their hair could be made that color.

Her eyes were wise from the start, but soft and beautiful. She often looked deep in thought. She practiced accomplishments in her head over and over before she debuted her final act. Often we could hear her through her monitor singing her ABCs to soothe herself to sleep. Or we'd find her secreted away on the stairs, going up a little and down a little until one day she could do the whole flight.

As Kennedy grew older, she had fully engaged parents, even though in many ways Dawson and I had grown parallel in the way we related to each other. Dawson was an amazing dad, and that helped to stabilize our home life and lessen some of the fights. Convinced she was going to be famous and on TV and the radio, Kennedy talked about it like it had already happened. "Mommy, I am eating my vegetables for when I am an Olympic swimmer," she frequently told us. Kennedy was a happy child, oblivious to all the disconnectedness around her. She exuded positivity and wanted desperately to spread it. When we were with her, it was impossible not to be infected by her happiness. The world was hers to conquer, and she wanted people in her life to help her do it.

EVEN THOUGH DAWSON and I were on a constant roller coaster, there were two things we had deeply in common. First, we could often be working on a project together with no effort, and second, we had a very robust, healthy sex life.

As our friends chose to hire workmen to solve or maintain any house issues, Dawson and I often set to work ourselves. Of course our finances didn't allow us to hire anyone, but when it came to painting, tiling, building, landscaping, or almost any kind of renovation, we worked well together. We loved it too. Our projects were a source of laughter and healing. We grew together in those moments, and we were good at transformations. As Kennedy got older and Tom was with us more often, they too benefitted from seeing Dawson and me endeavor together. In many ways there is no explanation for why Dawson and I could connect physically. At our absolute worst, however, even the slightest touch of our pinkies could ground me. And that became our thing. Whatever the argument and whatever the strife, eventually one of us would stick out a pinkie and we would slowly allow each other back in after that.

And as our friends were doing whatever they could to avoid physical contact and becoming stale in their marriages, Dawson and I truly enjoyed the magic of being together. It was a beautiful combination of excitement and exhilaration.

ꙮ *CHAPTER SIX*

AFTER KENNEDY WAS BORN, THERE WAS NO QUESTION in my mind that I wanted more children. It never occurred to me that I would have an only child. With the strong sense of insecurity about Tom not being truly mine, I deeply wanted Kennedy to have a sibling. I wanted her to have a full-blooded sibling because I envisioned that bond to be everlasting.

We had not planned Taylor per se, but we had not tried to prevent her either. So while our relationship was predictably unstable, which made it oddly steady, Dawson was still determined to be "done" with our marriage right when we found out that Taylor had been conceived. Sticking with our style of lunatic decision making, we not only stay married, but decided to build a house. Tom was nine and Kennedy was one. Life was unpredictable, but now that we were going to have three kids, a dog, and a work-from-home mom, our house had become too small and we needed more space. Dawson was stable at work and I wanted change.

The low level of anxiety I had once felt as a kid in front of a loud TV waiting for my dad to explode made sense to me. Further, I grew up with the constant underlying feeling that something wasn't quite right but that I had to move forward anyway. So here I was in a marriage that looked okay but felt rickety, and of course I continued to move forward. My ability to adjust made sense to me. I was comfortable in my familiar chronic instability, even if I was exhausted by it.

The truth is Dawson and I were excited to have Taylor.

And building a house was yet another project that we could do together.

DURING THIS PREGNANCY Taylor never settled in one place. She was very wiggly. With Taylor I gained fifty pounds. I failed every sugar test and was constantly on medical watch for something. Taylor took over my body. A foot in my side, her butt in my back, Taylor always let me know she was there.

It hadn't been the same with Kennedy. To conceive Kennedy, I monitored my periods. Sex was timely. She was overplanned. She had one spot in my belly and she planned to stay there until I forced her out. Unlike Kennedy, Taylor was a complete surprise. I allowed myself to dream a little with Taylor. She seemed to complete our family. We eagerly awaited her arrival, but Dawson and I knew we were done with kids once she came. Taylor was no solution to our instability, but I loved that I was going to have two of my own, and I loved that they would be sisters. Even better, they had a doting and protective older brother, half or not.

TIME PASSED REALLY quickly given everything that we had going on. Before we knew it, Kennedy was two, Tom was ten, the house was complete, and Taylor was born. Spring had sprung, and we were a family of five.

For all the speed with which Taylor arrived on the scene, her personality in life was much slower. "Come on, Taylor . . ." was often the last call before we walked out the door on any given morning.

"Mommy, I don't like to hurry." As slow as Taylor could be, her lingering allowed for endless discovery: a cloud shaped like a dinosaur, a puddle that looked like a cat, a pattern that could be recreated in paint. Taylor often picked up leaves and tucked them away in her pocket for a project she would do later.

If ever there were two more opposite kids, I gave birth to them—a realist and a dreamer, mirror images of the two parents who had created them.

As different as they were, as they grew older they had abundant interest in each other: "Taylor, what did you do in school today?" "Kennedy, how was your day?" "Hey, do you want to play American Girl dolls—no, let's play Uno." Peas in a pod. Together they played, laughed, and loved, always making room for Tom and Morgan.

SILLY AND ALOOF. Taylor had white-blond hair perfectly coiffed at her request, piercingly blue eyes, and flawless skin; when we went out, strangers often stopped to say what a gorgeous child Taylor was. A skip of my heart and a wave of uneasiness would ensue; couldn't they see that Taylor was kind? It was undeniable that Taylor was the right amount of chubby and cute, but she was so much more too. She had a gentleness of spirit and she had a connectedness within her that softened our family. Whatever loose ends Dawson and I still had were loosely tied for now. The birth of Taylor offered us a reminder of our love and a break from our dysfunction. These feelings of completeness were a welcome relief.

CHAPTER SEVEN

I KNEW THAT I WAS RASH IN MAKING MY DECISION TO marry Dawson. Still, my heart quivered when I met him. My knees got weak. He was tall, dark, and handsome. The opposite of my usual type. He was fast and fun. He was the life of the party. He was unpredictable. For all those reasons I convinced myself this time would be different.

Dawson and I were married by a justice of the peace. Dawson was born and raised Catholic, but had no ties to his religion except rigid memories of meaningless bible verses he'd recited. I was born and raised nothing. My mom Presbyterian and my dad Episcopalian, religion was just another disagreement my parents had never settled. We literally didn't talk about it or go through any motions on Christmas and Easter. We were not "believers" nor were we "nonbelievers"—we just weren't in the conversation about God *at all*. If you wanted something in your life, it was your responsibility to go get it. Dawson and I hadn't discussed church. Actually, we hadn't discussed a lot of things before we were married.

However, one crisis too many led us to longing for strength we didn't have. Dawson knew a life with religion; I was willing to follow his lead. So when Dawson and I discussed going to church, we just looked in the newspaper and chose the one that was having a "music Sunday," whatever that meant.

With our stresses mounting, we were open to a way of life bigger than us, but I was pretty new to all of it. Most Sundays I just sat and listened; other Sundays I spaced out and wrote a to-do list in my head. Very slowly the minister's words and sermons began to resonate with me. The minister kept referring to the wind. He cited the wind as a spirit. I liked the sound of that.

In all honesty, I was suffering deeply at this time, trying to sort through truth and illusion during the initial journey into Dawson's sobriety. When an alcoholic gets sober, there is a lot of truth unveiling, which can sometimes last for years. We were about two years in, and I often hurt from what I learned. Reconciling arguments with Dawson was better when we didn't actually talk. At times the simple gesture of touching pinkies felt like the one true thing in a vastness of falsehoods. At night we were tired, and all our words were really just defenses against each other's perceived wrongdoing. We were still working really hard to keep our marriage alive, seeing a few different types of therapists over the years, but neither of us stayed committed for too long. Church seemed like a comforting and effortless alternative.

But church was one hour a week and the rest of the time I was drowning in my own anger and regretting my short-sighted decision making. In the process of Dawson going to AA, I had taken up Al-Anon for myself. I had been going for about a year and had gotten myself a sponsor, but I was still the same struggling misfit. Every Tuesday night I would go to a meeting and every Tuesday I would leave feeling a part of a group, but eerily still lost and alone. Having children alters your perception on life. It alters your priorities. But for me it also gave me a window into love and joy that was entirely unfamiliar. I just didn't understand how that translated to being a married adult running a family, and I didn't want to pass on what my parents had inadvertently taught me. These groups gave belonging, a feeling that had eroded in me. But the groups were no substitute for a family. How could I make this work and belong in my life at home?

MY AL-ANON SPONSOR never pushed God on me or as they say in AA: "God as you understand Him." She would often say, "Embrace the mystery." Since I didn't know anything about God, it seemed acceptable to embrace the mystery; to me, it was *all* a mystery. She once told me that if I believed peanut butter was my higher power, I should pray to a jar of it. I was desperate for help, but never that desperate.

God seemed so great and so foreign to me. How was I supposed to give up my control to Him? I really didn't get it. I'm not the type to sit around waiting for things to happen. The wind was something that I didn't understand either—so big and forceful, yet also gentle and soothing. I never knew where it came from and where it went. Soon enough I was adopting it as my higher power because it seemed better than peanut butter and more tangible than some being I couldn't see.

The truth is, growing up a swimmer, Sundays were reserved for sleeping in. Fellowship, love, and support in a Christian way were not things you needed when you had a swim family. Accountability and unconditional support, friendly smiles, and generous acknowledgements from all ages were all around you on a pool deck. We were so committed to the sport, and we spent the better part of each week together. They were my support and being successful was my higher power. I was in control in the pool. What I put in, I always got out. So when I left college, I thought I was leaving behind just hard practices and tough meets, not unconditional love and respect. I was desperate to find meaning again. So, for the first time in my life, I was just trying to listen to people and hear what they had to say. Just sitting in the pews on Sunday gave me inner peace. It opened my eyes to boundless love and power beyond myself. At least that is what I took from the scriptures. Each speaker was a gift to nurture my inner self, but the messages were still so "out there." Each Sunday quieted the inner conversations I was having in my brain, mainly arguments with myself about my actions. Listening to other perspectives was a welcome change from my confused life at home and my overanalyzing nature.

Shortly into our church life beginning, Taylor was born, and shortly after that, Tom's life took a life-altering detour when he developed an autoimmune disease so rare it was hardly diagnosable. His illness only heightened our marital stress. We were juggling one child barely a year old, a two-year-old, and a paralyzed ten-year-old; mounting money problems with Dawson out of work again; and friendly "I told you so"s about our marriage. House projects and sex were not a stable foundation. We were crumbling.

Where my energy had been exhausted, the church community picked up my slack. Hot meals, a free babysitter, a carpool—everyone pitched in. My life was workable because people held me up with no questions asked. This was like my swim family, except I didn't have to go to practice. The more people reached out, the more humble and grateful I became.

The hard shell was being cracked whether I wanted it to or not.

I needed release from my own destructive thoughts, but I had so many trust issues. I didn't want another judgmental conversation with a friend. Or advice from someone who thrived on crisis. I was sure I could find people who would advise me to leave him. So I began to talk to the wind like the minister had recommended, and, sure enough, it talked back.

❧ CHAPTER EIGHT

WHEN DAWSON WAS "DONE," THERE WAS ALWAYS AN exhausting fight and a lengthy and angry negotiation and struggle with no result. The considerations of a divorce seemed endless and the cost too enormous. But when Tom got sick, it was different from the usual tirade of "I'm done, I'm leaving." There is no doubt he was probably done right before the illness, but lying in bed the night of its discovery, zapped of energy, Dawson began to cry. It was the second time he had cried that week. His body shook, and he covered his face as it began to get wet from tears. "He could have died," he said. It was true. Tom had been diagnosed with Guillain-Barré Syndrome, a rare autoimmune disease where your body eats your nerves. His case was even more rare; his nerves were eaten from the inside. There is no cure for it. There is no medicine to stop it. The disease takes its course, and whatever damage you are left with, you must rehabilitate and the nerves regenerate. It doesn't affect your brain, only your body.

Dawson had been back out of work for a few months. So instead of me, he had taken the drive to pick up Tom at school. It was nice to have him around with all the work around the house to manage—even if we weren't getting along. Taylor was starting to crawl, and Kennedy was grow-ing interested in exploring everything. Tom was struggling with school, slowly changing into a distant preteen at the age of ten. The grind of the fifteen-minute drive each way to pick up Tom had been wearing on me because I had to pack up the girls every time, so at least for today I had looked forward to avoiding it. It was not my town community and the pickup moms all knew I was the *step*mother. They whispered and stared.

By then Kennedy was a very busy three-year-old with a developing extroverted personality. She would talk to anyone and hold a lengthy conversation. She loved being around people, and held court for fairly large crowds. And Taylor, at fifteen months, wanted to be a full contributor to our family as well. Not knowing she was the baby, Taylor often struggled to keep up with everything her sister was doing, but Taylor's true affinity was to be with Tom. She could often be found snuggling up to him or showing off a newly learned skill for him.

School, sports, and activities kept us distracted until that day Dawson went to go pick up Tom.

As the kids started pouring out of all the elementary school doors and the noise levels began to rise—backpacks flying at parents, instrument cases being handed off—there stood Tom, the fifth grader, in his pajamas.

"It was a bad morning," Tom explained, anticipating Dawson's questions. "Mom couldn't get out of bed." Unless it was pajama day, the lack of proper clothing stood out in fifth grade. Today wasn't pajama day.

"We are going to her house," Dawson declared. "You need your lacrosse clothes, pads, and regular clothes." Tom hesitated.

Her house was literally walkable from the school, but

they drove because Dawson didn't want to spend even an extra minute lingering in her world. The yard outside Tom's mother's was always filled with untouched big plastic toys from early childhood. Their original color had faded, they were dirty, and most were broken. The front porch was filled with garbage and stacked empty wine crates. Often an empty wine bottle or two was outside the crate as well. The house door was unlocked when they got there.

At first Tom went in alone, but then, flustered, he came out empty-handed. Back in the car he begged Dawson to drive back to our house. Undeterred, Dawson dragged Tom back inside the house. It was ransacked. Shelves had fallen. Pictures of Dawson and Sara from when they were still married seven years prior were askew. This wasn't their marital house. Garbage littered the floor. Empty alcohol containers were everywhere. Old cigarette butts were scattered on the counters and the floors, and dog feces sat guiltily throughout the house, even in the clean laundry basket.

On the outside, Sara's life looked perfectly tended to. She was always immaculately dressed. Her nails impeccably painted, never chipped, never showing signs of having done a few loads of dishes. She was always ready to go out. Even on the soccer fields she managed stilettos.

We knew she was a mess on the inside. There were signs: Tom returning to us dehydrated, unkempt, and often extremely tired after three days with her. Time with Sara was either exhilarating and fun—life was a party—or it was dark and depressing. They could spend forty-eight hours in bed watching TV and barely eating. Tom told us odd stories of people he didn't know sleeping at the house on the weekend.

This, however, was more reminiscent of a crime scene.

Standing in horror, Dawson could barely muster a noise, and Tom had no explanation. The best Dawson could do was just try to hold in the shock until he got home and released it to me.

So when Tom's thigh began to hurt that afternoon, we were advised by his therapist and doctors that it was probably just stress. And the next day when the lethargy took hold, it was plausible that a bit of depression was taking over. The pediatrician passed it off as just one more thing in the "life of an active child." But after a few more days of worsening symptoms, Dawson began to worry.

Dawson took him back to the doctor and then to another. He was misdiagnosed by the first three doctors. Dawson eventually took Tom to an emergency room.

That day, the senior neurologist on call placed Tom in critical care for what would be five days and diagnosed him with Guillain-Barré Syndrome. With only the reassurance that we were lucky it wasn't worse, Tom was released home to our care.

I attacked this disease the way I used to attack an opponent in my swimming days. *Not today,* I used to say to myself. *You will not beat us today.* Now I looked at this boy in my care, biological son or not, and I told myself, *not today will he remain sick.* I had the fire in my belly I needed to survive and advance, just like I had my entire life until now.

Unfortunately, society fought me during his recovery. In the eyes of the already judgmental world around me, I wasn't his real mother. And the more social pushback I got, the harder I fought to fix Tom. I was undeterred by friends' questions, therapists' denials, doctors keenly observing from a distance, and the schools placing value on his mother regardless of what Dawson had seen at her house that day. It didn't matter how bad the signs were; the world didn't want to believe a mother could let a child endure such abuse. It was easier to believe Dawson was an absentee father with the "new life and new wife," even though none of that had been true. Sara went unquestioned.

Dawson and I applied for a bed at the closest children's hospital, and he was accepted. It was forty minutes away though. And it tore us in two different directions. Dawson was now splitting his time between searching for a job and time with the girls, and I split mine between time at home and time with Tom in the hospital. There just weren't enough hours in the day to give to anything or anyone else. And we grew resentful of each other as the forces of our life tore us apart.

After three months and very little fifth grade, Tom was released from his full-time hospital care. At the age of ten, almost eleven, he was in a wheelchair, with leg braces, a back brace, and two arm braces. Fourteen doctors met with us to explain that he had a fifty-fifty chance of ever walking again. Yet upon release, the doctors and therapists simply glossed over Sara's conveniently timed move to a second-floor apartment with no elevator. They simply guided Dawson to take full custody, handed us a prescription for a handicap license plate, and went about business as usual.

So without any fanfare, after years of battling in court to get custody without any success, Tom became ours full time. While Sara with her perfectly coiffed hair, precise makeup, and impeccably manicured nails called herself mom, I, with Taylor just a toddler and Kennedy a growing little girl, taught him how to once again button his clothes; wipe his bottom; use utensils; and complete his English, math, history, and Spanish work—all the while making sure that he got to physical therapy three days a week at the hospital and two days a week at home and that he was actually mothered. I fielded the school and doctor calls, got him on the special bus, baked cookies for the bake sale, managed the church fundraiser in his honor, and lugged the wheelchair and eventually the walker in and out of the back of the car with two little ones in tow.

I was keeping life moving forward, one foot in front of another like a drill sergeant, for my army of three kids, a dog, a job, and a husband—in that order.

IT'S IN THESE moments that I needed something to believe in. What kind of God lets this happen? Who do you trust in these times? The doctors certainly had led us in circles. Tom's therapist had missed all the warnings of neglect. The State Department of Children and Families wasn't interested in listening. In a world of abundant help and resources, why hadn't anything stopped this trajectory?

DAWSON ACCEPTED A job to get us financially on track; I just pushed forward. Still we kept showing up at church on Sundays. We kept our pinkies touching every once in a while. We kept our love in the sheets. We held on even though most days we probably could not have told anyone what we were holding on *to* exactly.

When the fights were bad enough to warrant an "I'm done!" Dawson moved down the hall. Those nights I was alone, I stayed on my side of the mattress. It was eerily cold on the other. There was no 5:30 a.m. alarm waking me up, but still my body rolled over at that hour. I suppose it rang somewhere else. The silence was my reminder of a restless night, a reminder of the absence of our healing touch; my fatigue and puffy eyes, a reminder of the tension.

In the mornings it was an effort to force myself out of bed at around six thirty. After our fights, the kids woke sheepishly too, but still had their usual morning demands:

"Mom, where is my favorite shirt?"

"Mom, can you help me brush my teeth?"

"There is no more toilet paper," someone would call from the bathroom.

"I can't find my science book."

"Brin, can you sign this permission slip?" Tom would ask.

The requests didn't end until all three of them left the house. The middle school bus came at seven fifteen, the nursery school drop-off was at eight, and Taylor's daycare drop-off was eight thirty. Three different schools, three different directions. Three different lives I had in my hands.

My weak and joyless smile was meant to distract the kids from my puffy eyes and blank stare. Mechanically, I got the laundry out of the dryer and handed off the blue shirt with the sparkly heart. I picked up the toothbrush and put the pea-size Crest dab onto it. I refilled the toilet paper stash, handed off the science book, and signed the permission slip. Then I headed downstairs where the details were different but the routine still the same. I poured the cereal, packed the lunches, found the right folders and books for the right bags, and pronounced the plan for the afternoon.

In between tasks, I fought back the water that would

slowly start to fill my eyes and bubble up. I never knew what
was making me the most upset—my insecurity, my pain, or
my exhaustion. The internal fight to figure it out only made
the lump in my throat bigger. With each turn to rinse a bowl
or fill a lunch, I could distract myself from the inevitable.
Just one minute at a time and soon I could let the tears fall.
The bus would come. The nursery school and daycare drop-
offs would pass. Then I would have a moment of silence.

DAWSON'S NEW JOB worked him long hours, and my responsibilities at home were drowning me. Unable to connect,
Dawson went his way and I went mine. We operated in parallel
universes. His hours were filled with a commute, a stressful
job, and a son in peril. Mine were filled with rehab centers,
doctors, insurance paperwork, two little ones, and an ailing
dog. I was in control, but I was a robot. We each just put one
foot in front of the other to get by. Whether we liked it or
admitted it, we still needed each other, yet betrayal and anger
were corroding us. Life was uncomfortable but predictable. If
it was not, I was sure to fall apart. Dawson hated predictability
and regularity. I hated how emotionless I was becoming. And
I hated his judgment and I hated my judgment. We simply
were at odds. And yet each Sunday we could come together
and sit in a pew with pinkies attached—holding on with the
thread that was still alive between us. And slowly my tears
would wash away a layer of anger, enough for me to drop my
head on his shoulder and slow myself to rest, sinking into his
body if only for an hour.

⟋ CHAPTER NINE

MORGAN, OUR DOG, BROUGHT UNCONDITIONAL LOVE TO our house of turmoil, and it wasn't just the wag of her tail when we came home. Just like Kennedy, Morgan comforted me endlessly.

Like all of us in the house those days, she had her own personality. Morgan was not one to be left out. She often put her nose right in your lap, looking to get some attention, and if the nose didn't work, next was her paw in your lap. She was an eighty-five-pound lapdog who humbled us, and Dawson and I both knew it. We would be in the middle of a fight and mention to each other that "even Morgan doesn't want to hear us."

Let me take a step back; I am not much of an animal person. I don't love every dog, I hate cats, and small rodent-type pets are a "no way" in my house. I don't even care for fish. Those days, I wasn't even sure I was a people person half the time. In my house, there was a very high chance that I would throw you away or reupholster you if you didn't speak up for yourself.

It was Dawson who actually had taken Morgan to the specialist when we realized she had problems. In fact, it was on the heels of discovering I was pregnant with Kennedy that we were also told Morgan had severe degenerative issues. She wasn't even one yet, and we either had to fix her or put her down.

Our family needed her comfort, not more crisis. Something about her presence was peace inducing. But more critically Morgan was the fulfillment of a promise Dawson had made to Tom during his divorce process. When Dawson and Sara had split up, Tom had lost his dog. Morgan was the replacement. It was too devastating to think of explaining the issues to Tom. I wouldn't do it.

We felt we had no real option but to embark on what became four major surgeries. While I grew in my pregnancy, Morgan was slowly being surgically put back together. When Kennedy came, Morgan was not jealous. They would lie down together, Morgan and Kennedy. The two of them had a bond. Tom had also found comfort in Morgan. She really did offer a lot of love.

As time passed and Morgan was doing better, Taylor came and Tom got sick. Easily adjustable, Morgan went with the flow each time something changed to accommodate the differences in the house.

It wasn't too long before Tom got better and the girls got bigger. Suddenly Morgan took a turn for the worse. More lows than highs became her norm.

Morgan was my dog. My company. My family. She protected my heart, and she loved my children.

I struggled with my faith. I struggled with my marriage. I struggled with my kids. Now I struggled with losing my dog.

After all the surgeries for her degeneration, and the gentle care, and four leg surgeries, we still couldn't fix Morgan. Shortly after we'd come to terms with Tom's wheelchair, the kid who might not walk again was walking and his leg braces were gone. Precisely when there was a brief respite from drama and stress, Morgan was diagnosed with cancer.

The medications to slow the tumor growth weren't working. So we made an appointment with the vet. There was just no way to have a dog her size with only two working legs. Dawson stayed with Morgan through her final moments. I kissed her good-bye. We left having asked for her ashes. Dawson didn't know why, but he knew he wanted them. Flooded with tears and sadness, all I could think of in the car was where we should bury her. It was on Martha's Vineyard that she was happiest, so we agreed to bring the kids and spread her ashes in the place she loved most.

The truth is, I still wasn't sure I knew what love was. I knew my mom loved us but her love was in execution and function. My dad said he loved us but his love was in words. My siblings and I loved through protecting each other and being there for each other. We most certainly didn't talk about anything. My first marriage, a repetition of my childhood, my second marriage still an unknown. What was love supposed to be? I guess I could have just mirrored the love I had for my kids, but with your kids the expectations are different. I believed I had no out. I had no way to detach, no way to run the way I did with everyone else in the world.

Our life was a chain of unraveling events, and I was crumbling with every loss. I trusted only that another shoe would eventually drop. Even my friends were worn out from the drama. My attitude often had an agenda, and it was to control my family. But what control do you really have over anyone? And who was I to decide how people should live their lives? Trying to make things happen my way felt like I was a drowning person clinging to the lifeguard rescuing me —I was on the verge of taking everyone down with me, drowning all of us.

Again, I was faced with the question of what to believe in if people weren't the answer. On top of everything, I had just lost my one true animal love, Morgan. With her the answers had been easy. She was always there for me—for better or for worse. For richer or for poorer. In sickness and in health.

CHAPTER TEN

SOME NOISES ARE JUST COMFORTING. THEY REMIND YOU that you are not alone. No wag of the tail. No thump of her body lying down. No bark as the mailman came to the door. My comfort was gone.

So when Dawson and I had walked in the door from the kindergarten fundraiser that fatal night, there was nothing to comfort me with unconditional love. I was only reminded that the party had been a good diversion from resenting each other. As much as we disagreed, we had grown into a pattern of moving forward by simply attending events or taking life's curves by each other's sides. To the outside world our smiles portrayed the perfect couple. On the inside we were just going through routines and familiar motions.

Somewhere in the frenzy of getting ready to go to bed, with the miserable recollection that one half of our queen-sized sleeper would remain empty that night, the phone rang again. The phone never rang after nine at night. My anxiety heightened at the sound of the first ring and one look at the number on the Caller ID. It was late and I had *already* talked to Claire. She knew Dawson was home because I had abruptly cut off our conversation earlier when he had arrived. I sensed the words on the line were going to bring bad news because calls after a certain hour are never good.

‿ᕗ

I HAD CONFIDED in Claire about Dawson's divorce decree earlier. I hoped she was checking on me just in case, but I didn't feel confident in my hope. It was after ten. This was not normal, and I had nowhere to go for a private conversation—even though Dawson was down the hall, sounds carried in our house, so I jumped into our master bathroom.

Her voice halted me. Hesitant but firm, she said that Taylor had told her daughter Mackenzie something odd. "Tom's bottom looked like a hot dog and went pee pee in your mouth when you sucked on it." I muttered out loud, "Uh-huh, yeah, hmm, okay." All the while inside saying, "Okay, we can figure this out." I repeated out loud over and over, "This isn't possible." My body tensed as the conversation went on. The bathroom felt like it was closing in on me, and Claire gave me no room for denial. I felt trapped.

My head was exploding near the toilet. Except for the sound of my own racing pulse in my ears, I couldn't hear much. I didn't feel much either. My fight-or-flight response was temporarily frozen. And then in a flash I was overcome, and my senses surged from numb into hyperdrive.

I heard the door to Tom's room open; suddenly my ears were bionic. He was retiring for the night. The two girls were finally asleep. Stumbling to articulate what I hadn't yet digested myself, I grabbed Dawson from down the hall and brought him into the bathroom. At that moment it felt like the bathroom itself lacked room enough for even oxygen, let alone the two of us and this topic. My adrenaline surged again. If there was a God, he certainly wasn't in that bathroom either.

Here we now were, Dawson and I, broken and still breaking, trapped and left to discuss the unthinkable as if we were a team.

I nervously repeated everything Claire had said, the words surreal coming out of my mouth. The accusation pierced even my ears as I heard it through my own voice. Crisis-cultivated decisions were all that we could make at that point. Steps were not being planned. Dawson and I were doing what we had come to perfect. Our bodies were just instinctually moving forward and parallel together. It was as if we had an invisible to-do list just for this scenario.

Experts say in a trauma your body automatically goes into fight, flight, or freeze. We were a molded combination of fight and flight in these moments. At any given moment each one of us changing from fight to flight and vice versa, neither one of us in the same mode at the same time.

We swiftly moved to the girls' room, confronting Taylor who sleepily repeated the same exact story we had already heard. At three, it was nervous sounding. She smiled in her awkwardness. She giggled at her use of words. Next we drew Kennedy from a rare deep sleep. We brought her gently downstairs and placed her on the couch. It was hard to pry her awake, but she soon came out of her sleepy haze. We asked her what they had told the babysitter, Mackenzie. Sitting up instantly as if she knew the seriousness of her previous words, she, too, repeated the identical declaration. Dawson tested her—"That is a big statement, Kennedy. Will you face Tom on it?" With maturity and strength beyond that of a four-year-old, she agreed. Her thinned-out little body held firm in her chair while we waited for both Dawson and Tom to return. She showed no signs of doubt or worry. I didn't coddle her in those moments as we waited. She sat independent and ready.

Dawson returned, accompanied by a reticent Tom, who slumped into a chair. Without hesitance Kennedy looked straight into his face—"You made me suck your bottom." His face turned red and his body contorted. He denied it. He fumbled an excuse, saying that he did raspberries into their stomach during the tickle game. He moved his head side to side nervously, hoping the story would stick. Tom's previously handicapped arms and legs showed complete function while he squirmed like he had all his nerves loose and ready. Was it fight or flight?

The room's silence grew in meaning. Uncomfortable adjustments by everyone, but no real noise. It hung in the air for what seemed like hours.

Tom broke the silence with another denial, but he was growing more uncomfortable on the footstool, his legs wiggling ferociously now. Kennedy sat on the couch an inch or two elevated from him. I sat on a single chair and Dawson sat on the other end of the couch. No one was close, physically or mentally. Kennedy was in fight. Tom longed for flight. At that moment though, we were all in freeze.

Just as the silence was killing us—another break. "Mommy, I promise I am telling the truth." Then it happened; Tom conceded, "Okay I did it, but only once."

The pace suddenly changed. Immediately there was hustle. Dawson started barking orders:

"Brin, call Tom's therapist, Dr. Anderson."

All I heard was, "You have reached the after-hours call line of Dr. David Anderson."

Click. I didn't need a voicemail.

"Dawson, I'm going to call the pediatrician."

A live voice: "You have reached the emergency line for Dr. Bill, what is your emergency? . . . Uh-huh, okay. The doctor will call you back." I can't remember what I said. It was of no consequence in that moment anyway.

The ring of the phone would now terrorize our house for weeks to come. But that night Dr. Bill soon called back, patiently heard what we knew, and advised us to take Tom out of the house. He would call the authorities in the morning and see the girls first thing. For the next hour, however, packing, loud voices, tears, a fury of chaos prevailed over our house. Disbelief. In the dead of the night, Dawson was back in the car, moving Tom to his mother's. As the silence returned, my head was dizzy with disbelief. Darkness was setting in.

Within the hour Dawson had returned home, and that night he also returned to our bed. We did not sleep that night. We just held each other. We just were.

THERE IS A reason why crisis therapy is six weeks in length. It has to do with our biological ability to cope. In those six weeks there is no healing happening. One is just alive. I was alive physically. I'm not sure I was alive mentally. Waves of grief would wash over me and anything could cause its trigger. I'm pretty sure in that time of need we can experience all five stages of grief at once, but it's like a tsunami of emotion, so identifying any one particular stage and working through it is impossible. If I wasn't hyperangry, I was completely numb.

It took two weeks for the evaluations and therapists to finish. Swirls of questions. Every parenting decision called into question by the professionals and the police. We were all being investigated. In the same time frame Tom had been arrested and expelled. Two weeks of mistrust swirling between Dawson and me and spilling out everywhere. Two weeks of defensiveness, arguments about how to handle the now-large legal issues. How to embrace the offenses, the consequences, the punishment. Two weeks to begin what would be an extreme outpouring of money and two years of unraveling. We were at that moment no longer parallel. We were no longer on the same team. It was each man for himself, or maybe we were offense and defense. There was no path for us to follow from those that came before us. Only 10 percent or less of abuse cases are caught during their actual time of occurrence. When they looked at Dawson and me, they saw the father of three children in pain and me the mother of only the victims. Of course we would be divided and broken. Having no similar scenarios in their respective practices, the experts set quite natural limitations on us and offered advice for a divorce on more than one occasion. It was a common and understandable framework to fit us into. No one had ever seen anything like this. I'm sure they felt their words were understanding and even sympathetic: *Of course they will divorce. The odds are entirely stacked against them*, they must have thought. Somehow, somewhere, deep in my soul though, divorce was still not the option.

⁓

EARLY IN THE investigation we sat in a small conference room at the state agency which investigates abuse, Child Guidance. Around a table that could fit eight, we seemed like a group bigger than the room. Mismatched chairs were provided to accommodate the ten of us who were now sitting in the space. Tense and suffocated, Dawson and I waited as awkward staff filed into the room after their Sexual Assault Rescue Team (SART) interview with Kennedy. We had been interviewed separately as well. By now it was clear they were not only looking into Tom but also trying to make sure neither Dawson nor I knew about this abuse prior to its discovery. Everyone was being vetted.

Of all the authorities, there were only two men in the room: the police officer and Dawson. Faces filled with apprehension, bodies all a bit antsy, anxious from a conversation no one wanted to start. Tapping pencils and very surface small talk filled the time as we waited longer. I could have lifted a small house and moved it a mile down the road by the time the first words were spoken. My adrenaline and trigger instincts were readying me to fight. I figured I knew what the answers would be; Tom had gone on to admit what he'd done. Anxiously, I was just ready for this *routine* meeting to be over; surely by now we would not be hearing new news. I was resolved to having already heard the worst.

With a heavy sigh the representative from the Department of Children and Family Services who had just completed the interview said, "Mr. and Mrs. Miller. I am sorry we are here today. We had a good talk with Kennedy. She is a wonderful child . . ." Her words droned on. ". . . We know there was at least one penetration." Wait! What? She had my attention now!

"Most likely more. We do not need to interview Taylor. We have all we need from Kennedy. Do you have any questions? The people here today are willing to help your family in any way possible." What? Tension in my head created a bomb ready to explode; I was no longer ready to fight—I had kill streaming through my veins.

I felt Dawson squeeze my hand under the table. I didn't even realize we were holding hands. Prior to that squeeze, when I could look over, I saw his face go white with shock. His reaction quickly focused on the implications to Tom from the now-set-into-evidence video of Kennedy's interview. His body was on autopilot to defend but oddly still gentle with the handhold. My mouth dropped open and I released a primal, haunting, terrorizing scream that silenced Dawson's voice. The representatives regrouped, sitting up a little more attentively now. "Mrs. Miller," one of them said, "I know this is hard on you. It is also hard on Mr. Miller. You need to get yourself under control, and we cannot let the girls see or hear you this way."

CHAPTER ELEVEN

THE WORLD WENT BLACK, AND MY EYES WORKED BUT they didn't see. Things were floating in front of me. Or I was floating in front of things. My body tightened. My muscles clenched. My head got a slight ache, and I didn't know if the tears or the fist would come first. There was a scream inside my head that seemed so loud it could shake the earth, but it didn't come out anymore. The water started to surround my eyes and my eyeballs got a little painful and frozen. My face seemed like it may have been disconnected from my body and the darkness turned to brightness. More screams came out and simultaneously the tears started to fall. My body crumbled to the floor, and the pain set in like the moment after a baseball bat hits your head, heart, and then throat. At that precise moment, in all the horror I thought, *What did I do wrong? How did I fail my children?* My nose was dripping, my eyes were soaked, and my hands were wet from wiping both. I was stuck here on the floor unable to budge even my smallest body part.

Then it all stopped. *Oh no, not me. This isn't going to be me!*

When I could formulate a word, I was saying, "no, no, no," but in my head I knew it was a resounding "yes."

I imagine the feelings are similar to when a doctor tells you you have cancer. Or when the coroner tells you it's your child, parent, or best friend who died. I imagine it is the same when you miscarry or when you have been told you can't have children. Or when the murderer goes free for lack of evidence or when the arrest doesn't happen because the victims were too young to tell a clear story. First you want to fight, then you want to run, and eventually you freeze.

EXTRAORDINARILY AWFUL EVENTS happen in life, and because we don't always talk about them, we never know who they happen to. When they happen to you, there is no way to escape them. You can't buy your way out of them as a long-term solution. They come with you if you run. At first this awful event defined me—then it redefined me.

At the bottom of this black hole, which seemed like the valley of death I had heard about on Sundays, I wanted to know how this had happened. Was there a God? Because if there was, I wanted to talk! I had a few questions I wanted answered, and I thought I had waited long enough. That's not the way it works though. God doesn't wear a watch.

AT THE VERY break of each morning, right at the moment my eyes opened, I wondered if the news was all really a bad nightmare. As my brain became alert, the veil lifted, and the crying hangover and the exhaustion left in the adrenaline's wake reminded me of the truth and of our new reality. My marriage was even further broken. My kids were traumatized. All of us were in complete shock.

Yet life just kept happening. I *hated* that life kept happening. I needed a moment—just a little breather. I was resentful that the sun came up.

In the wake of tragedy, there is always a team of people put together to disperse the bad news and its details. Usually there are news blurbs in local papers, or church bulletins. Maybe an interview with a grieving family member. This is, more often than not, not the case in sexual abuse situations. These are private family matters.

Agreeing that public knowledge would do us more harm than good, we confided in only the people who had to know, like family, doctors, and certain school administrators; further, the people who we knew could keep it silent or by law *had to* keep it silent. It was a short list.

Even if we had wanted to, we did not have the full picture to tell anyone anyway. It would be two years before we uncovered the better part of the lies and deceitful stories.

Days passed and I often pulled the covers over my head one minute longer, two minutes longer . . . until there were no more minutes to be had. I fought with daylight. Fought reality. I abandoned my burgeoning faith. There was no fellowship to be had. This was our private hell.

There was too much to digest. So much raw information being told to me. Half the days I felt sick, and the other half I cried about what made me sick.

When I could, I managed a meeting with our minister. He was awkward at best with women, oversized and loud himself. He was the kind of guy who was deep inside but had no clue how to show it unless it was in a self-deprecating way. I liked him though. He was the kind of person who I didn't have to nurture. He was easy to be close to because it was all about faith and not at all about friendship. He was the one whose sermons on the wind had so resonated with me. He had opened my heart if only for an hour each Sunday. He had even baptized me the previous year. He had a deep understanding of loss because he too had experienced it, yet didn't seek to intertwine our stories because he understood and respected that loss is so personal. As much as there are universal feelings, each trial is its own. Our faith was perfect being parallel.

"Brin," he said, "you have got to get an antianxiety drug or you are going to die. Not the light kind either. Go for the heavy-duty stuff or you won't make it." *Okay*, I nodded, unsure of how to explain this to my doctor. Walking out of the meeting, he handed me a book on meditation that he told me to read and do, then reiterated the strong suggestion for sedatives. All I wanted was to know if this was what God intended for me and why. I left with no answers.

CHAPTER TWELVE

EACH NEW DISCOVERY OF TOM'S HIDDEN ACTS WAS LIKE his own shoebox of thrown-out moments. He had lost track, amid all the lies, of what exactly had been done to the girls. The now-revived memories began to weave an album of terror right under our own roof. Pictures no parent ever wants to hear about, let alone have taken with their kids. All our picture-perfect choreographed moments now seemed tarnished. The joy of family time had been killed by the revelations of the before or after.

With an animal instinct like a mother lion, most of the time I was in save mode with the girls. Each day releasing them to school was an effort in great courage. I couldn't shake the damage, and I couldn't navigate the anger. I still hadn't found a way to slow life down enough to feel grounded. My brain mirrored a gerbil on a wheel running to nowhere, unable to get off. If their brother could do this, what could the world around us do?

I reevaluated every friend based on whether they could be trusted to maintain our privacy or not. It was such a heavy burden of knowledge because using it as gossip wouldn't hurt Dawson and me as much as it would hurt Kennedy and Taylor. We didn't need anyone adding to the hate for Tom either. There was enough already. We debated before talking to anyone about any of the littlest things. Of course our families were told. On my side, it was easy for them to cut Tom out of their lives. On Dawson's side it was complicated at best. Each family member was left to their own decisions about Tom, and those were not all the same.

Then there were the babysitters. Clearly, they already knew because they were the first in the chain of events that night. Which led to Claire finding out. Which is ultimately how we heard. It's hard to imagine that we missed the warning signs. Shortly after we found out, one of Tom's first therapists actually wrote me an email saying that she had reviewed her notes and there were no warning signs and that she was sorry. In the aftermath of it all, I'm glad I never responded. I don't think my communication would have been too cordial. *Sorry*. What does that even mean in a situation like this?

There were times the truth was too heavy for me to carry alone. One day in church I was just standing around after service when a friend asked me how I was. I didn't hold it in. All the tears just burst from my eyes and the words burst from my mouth. Next thing I knew her arms were around me and I was in a tight, warm, and loving embrace. The hug might have lasted a few minutes, but her friendship and dedication to me has endured.

Thanksgiving had come and gone in a haze. We tried to find blessings, but during that time Tom was also being removed from "holding" to a school in Utah. Dawson had researched and orchestrated his move. He spent desperate days and nights focused on the solution for Tom. It wasn't the right place or the wrong place—it was the only place. The juvenile justice system wasn't set up for the serious and heinous nature of his crimes, and he was not an adult at the age of thirteen. While Dawson was focused on sparing Tom,

I spent desperate days listening to the girls reveal every "secret" they had been warned to keep and nights trying to wrap my brain around it all.

IT'S HARD TO choose which days were the worst, but one particularly difficult day, there were no parking spots at karate. I had to deal with the frustrating circle around the block, having to take three left-hand turns through at least one stoplight. It was no more than five hundred yards, but a ten-minute circle all the same. I dropped the girls in front, making it safe and easy for them.

What was actually safe and easy anymore? I stayed to make sure they were in the door. Then I began my mission to find a parking spot. Ironically, I had interviewed the karate instructor for Tom, hoping it would help him gain strength after his paralysis. Tom wasn't interested though. So now here I was with the girls, using karate as a way for them to gain strength, maybe even establish the meaning of boundaries. *Oh God, the boundaries that had been lost.* Every thought could be its own trigger. No day without them.

At that moment, though, all I could focus on was parking, and then for forty-five minutes I would be able to rest in complete silence. I just needed to close my eyes and lay my head back, shutting out the thoughts of each horrifying story. The best I could do for myself and anyone was to focus on my three left turns and parking the car.

Just as I was pulling into a spot, the cell phone call came in. I was startled out of my daze with the first ring. It was Utah, which was now synonymous with "something to do with Tom." I hesitated, knowing that picking up meant less time to recharge my battery, but the adrenaline had already started to flow in my body and the anxiety created a shake. I had gotten the prescription for Xanax as my minister suggested; it was not quite the hard stuff but at least promised some relief. *I guess I should try to start taking it*, I thought in that moment. I was pretty jumpy; I really needed to force myself to allow medical relief. *I'll put it on the list of things to do when I get home.*

Tom's therapist spoke without hesitation. He tended to launch his statements at you. Maybe he was always breaking really disgusting news, and it was his way of getting through it. I didn't know him well and I didn't want to. "Brin, are you in a place where you can talk?" As his first words came out, I felt the jolt and wondered if I'd just hit the cement barrier with my car. One look at the gear, though, and I realized I was still in park. Every time I thought I had heard it all, there was more. It was impossible to imagine what I would hear on any given day. Really, I just couldn't imagine any new, unfolding detail. When he was done with what I had come to hear only as "Blah, blah, sexual exploration, your underwear, blah, blah, masturbation, blah," I thought, *Okay, tomorrow, I'll get new underwear.* Even my clean laundry was dirtied.

TUCKING AWAY THE tears and the shakes, hiding behind sunglasses, and talking slowly to avoid activating the growing emotional lump in my throat at pickup, I became a pro at disconnecting from my surroundings and floating through exchanges after school and at activities. There was still dinner to serve and a nighttime routine to observe. The days still kept passing without my permission.

Which meant months passed too. Therapy twice a week for both girls, therapy once a week for me, therapy once a week for our marriage—endless calls to Utah. Private phone and Skype therapy sessions with Tom because I was his only maternal figure who could help them piece together his life. I even had conference calls sitting in the car of the school parking lot while the girls were home with the sitters. Therapy and discovery seemed endless.

When I lay down, vivid images of Tom abusing the girls haunted me. I didn't want to close my eyes. Yet when I couldn't fight sleep any longer, I slipped into dreams of beating him until he was unrecognizable. The days were bad and the nights were worse.

The pediatrician even asked, "Brin, are you sleeping?"

There was no use in lying. It was obvious in my face. I answered, "No, not much these days. Can you tell?"

Caring deeply, he assured me, "You need to get some sleep. Can you take anything to help you?"

Feeling the humor in how obvious this was, I said, "I was given a prescription for Xanax for some anxiety issues a while back—I guess I could try that."

Without hesitation he responded, "You will need your sleep. Take them." My eyes flooded with tears as I walked out of the appointment. I was grateful for those people who were able to see beyond what I portrayed to the outside world. Any display of kindness made tears of gratitude flow. The people who knew our tragedy were incredibly dedicated to us, and it was a form of love I instinctually wanted to reject. Our network of caregivers was small, but they attended to us without agenda or judgment. They just had our delicate lives in their hearts and never let us feel let go.

I was uplifted in those *genuine* and real moments. People were so unselfish and loyal. I didn't know why, and I struggled to feel worthy.

Here I was day after day, uncovering and discovering what was *real* and *actual* in my life. Each memory now complete with the parts of the picture I wasn't meant to see or know. I was consumed with feelings about anything genuine and anything loving as really a load of crap. The lies swallowed me whole when I thought about them too long.

IN THAT DISCOVERY, what was revealed was that over the course of eight months, Tom had been waking the girls up in their room and trapping them in for the abuse. It was happening in our house; it was impossible to avoid feeling violated by this. In all our looking back, we reviewed everything we could to search for the signs we had missed. After Tom had gotten most of his mobility back, he began to have a harder time with school and socializing. While he had friends and was progressing in school, something seemed to be off. He was angry. We thought we understood, so we had actually moved him to a more teen male–focused therapist, and we tried to remain open and close with him. But he was pushing back hard. He was becoming defiant. There were signs, a little lie here and there. He avoided schoolwork and got a few detentions, even, for missed work, rejected doing physical therapy, and had had a fight at swim practice. He had even gotten caught on the computer a few times looking at porn. We were aware and sympathetic to his struggles. We thought we were helping. His increased focus on me became a bone of contention between Dawson and me. He often told Dawson stories about how mean I was, or how he had done the things I had asked of him and I was being "too hard on him." Now here we were learning of his real agenda. He had manipulated us all.

Before all this happened, I already had so many feelings of loss associated with my dad, my first marriage, Dawson's sobriety. I was angry. At least growing up, I had never doubted my mother's love, even though it came with so much control. I often felt she loved me even more when I had problems for her to fix. My dad always said that he loved me. He never missed a day, but his mental and physical absence didn't actually feel like love as much as he said it. Deep in my gut something always felt strangely incomplete in my childhood relationships. I knew I carried through in finding similarly incomplete relationships in my adulthood. And now I had two little girls who would wonder themselves about how love was supposed to work. Tom had played them. He swore them to secrecy and told them this is what brothers did.

So here I was, engulfed in a world of unraveling deceit and hate, struggling to stay afloat with hope, and cloaked in unprecedented support. How?

There were no hospital support groups for moms of raped toddlers. There were no anonymous weekly get-togethers to join. No fundraisers to get behind the cause. No awareness campaigns. Our lives were, as the experts reminded us, "forging new paths through unknown and highly rare circumstances." We were the "lucky" ones who had stopped the abuse and gotten help for everyone. As overcome as I was with wanting to push everyone away, our world embraced us and cloaked us in love; but love that grew from hate was confusing and made my head spin trying to figure it out.

CHAPTER THIRTEEN

WE HAD EXPERTS. THERAPISTS, PSYCHIATRISTS, DOCTORS, the pediatrician, clergy, lawyers, school administrators, teachers, and even court-appointed representatives. It wasn't sustainable. There wasn't enough time or money to have so many professionals in our lives. They told us that the more we knew about what had happened, the more we could help heal all three children. It was tricky though. Aside from Dawson and me, everyone had their own interests to represent. And you don't just ask a three- and four-year-old what had happened. Tom was so disassociated from his own behavior, he was unclear to listen to; his stories kept changing. Absolutely everything had to be explored, however. Every sexual scenario had to be gently asked about and worked through with Kennedy and Taylor. Simultaneously there were the discoveries from Tom. Who had he told? What had he done to each girl? What had he had them do together? What had he made them do to each other? Who else had he brought in? What other friends and households had been affected? What other little sisters? We kept spinning in this Who-What-Who-What circle.

The girls' side and Tom's side of the stories painfully came together to create one full picture that had been our unknown reality all along. Every word was a component to the radioactive bomb that had just exploded, leaving behind microexplosions every day.

I would often go back to the beginning and relive in my

head every full step Tom had made over ten years. I didn't even know him all ten years, but I tried to analyze him anyway. Piecing together the real story meant rewriting how our life had unfolded. Remembering things now with the whole truth attached was blasting my heart into fractions.

It turns out there are three therapeutic schools for problem sexual behavior in the United States. Something I never knew or needed to know before. Dawson had researched all three, visited two, and decided on one. The work Tom was doing there with his therapists helped us to shed light on his life at his mother's. We had certainly been aware of some things prior and had reported them to various therapists and doctors, but what we'd known was only just the surface of his neglect. Now we had to listen to tales of how Tom and friends were unsupervised by Sara or their parents who were drinking upstairs instead of parenting downstairs. Those same kids came around the house regularly and had unbridled access to the internet, paid TV, and inappropriate movies. Tom endured frequent adult all-night parties, often waking up with strangers sleeping around the house on chairs and couches. Then rushed mornings of Tom getting his mom out of bed because he was late to school and arriving on an empty stomach to his classroom seat. Rushed showers together to get clean, even after he was ten years old. Rummaging through piles of clothes on the floor, smelling each item to see if the pile was clean or dirty. Life was one big scramble, which finally ended the day Dawson picked Tom up and found him still in his pj's. Now it made sense that he was taking lunch from the underprivileged line. Now it made sense that he often had bags under his eyes from exhaustion and his schoolwork was suffering. As if what we had known already wasn't bad enough.

The work at this new school also included psychological tests, lie detectors, advisors, sealed files, and more gut-wrenching discovery that formed more disillusionment. Sobriety kills a lot of friendships, so we already had a rare social life. My sadness and desperation made me unfit for public life. I wanted to get out from underneath this pain. It was killing me. I would spend nights crying after I put the girls down to sleep. If Dawson was home, I would ask him to forgive my extra glass of wine, and I would try with whatever I could to drown out the noise and anger in my head.

DAYS PASSED INTO weeks and weeks passed into months. Life had hit such a low that the things Dawson and I used to argue about seemed completely inconsequential now. The girls were slowly getting some sleep again, and that helped to energize them. They were so young that they didn't even understand much of what had happened, so our goal was to quiet the trauma and start to rebuild their trust one moment at a time. Some safe people were in place for the girls. Dawson and I had created scripted answers about Tom's disappearance. Believe it or not, some things were actually easier. Dawson could no longer blame me for anything in regard to Tom. We had almost no interactions anymore with Sara. I had only two kids to wake and dress—both mine—and only two schools to get them to. Having two was in many ways easier than three. Even though we were clouded by a fog, a huge category 5 storm had lifted. I clung to these small mercies as the tiniest consolations.

One thing I had started to embrace was the miracle in us

finding out. In abuse cases, early intervention is everything for the life of the survivors. On October 20, 2011, two teenage girls told one of their mothers, and that mom had the courage to call us immediately, and Kennedy had the courage to face her attacker head-on, and we had the courage to listen. At any moment the chain of discovery could have broken. And it didn't. So the abuse was over and everyone was getting help. This nugget kept me from feeling helpless many lonely nights.

Our inner circle was really about four people for me and one or two for Dawson. They checked in on us every day at first. They called to make sure we had a shoulder to cry on or to listen to us repeat and process the newest unveiling. Each of them took turns making sure I didn't spend too much time alone or that Dawson and I didn't spend too much time together. No matter how busy their lives, my four friends made time for me. Anna took me out on walks; Britt came with me to court every session and drove me home, putting me back together every time; Joan was on call literally every day in person and over the phone; and Claire made sure I ate and also called or texted every day. They were my team.

Weekly visits to doctors and therapists for the girls also meant check-ins for me. Each physician took the extra time during the appointment with Kennedy or Taylor to let me release the tear or two that I was holding back for this reason or that reason—even no reason. We were surrounded by this mighty network of strength, and yet we had little to give. It was often hard to comprehend. Was it sympathy or love? The last thing I wanted was someone feeling sorry for me, but I had lost track of my ability to judge things anymore.

There was but one instance where a little bit of sympathy

would work in our favor. I had called the chief of police to beg him to keep the arrest out of the local paper. The police report is published every week. I couldn't handle the publicity. I envisioned newscasters standing outside our door looking for the exclusive interview. It was a small town. Social busy-bodies live for this type of information. I humbled myself to a pathetic mess of tears to make sure our problems weren't published. It was as much for me as it was the girls. He must have found a soft spot in his heart because against official police policy there was no story announced in the paper. No whispers as we walked down the street. No gossip to be passed as we stood at the bus stop waiting for the girls to come and go from school. We just took one step at a time each day and pretended like life was disrupted because of some poor unchangeable choices Tom had made. He was away at school because that was now "where he needed to be."

Occasionally we were confronted by a deeper question about where Tom had gone: a mother of one of Tom's friends, a schoolteacher who worked at our club—people who cared but would never make the inner circle—they all got the standing response of "he presented problems that were beyond our ability to help. He is where he needs to be." This was our short and polite way of shutting down the conversation and avoiding more questions. When we did finally venture to go out again, Dawson and I became good at changing the topic to small talk or simply finding an excuse for a polite exit to another conversation. We were protecting the safety of what was left of the family.

When we were out with our pinkies connected, Dawson and I didn't leave each other's sides. Without much effort we eventually circled back to operating on the same team. Divorce lawyers' cards were tucked away for another day; the perfect combination of fight and freeze holding us inexplicably together.

CHAPTER FOURTEEN

FOR A LONG TIME IT FELT LIKE THE MUNDANE PARTS OF our life went unnoticed. Our worries and concerns on marriage, kids, jobs, and money were completely buried in the rubble of the storm Tom had cast. I have no idea how the bills got paid or whether the beds were made on most days. That's the irony in tragedy: you temporarily lose track of how life moves forward. I guess we managed through.

If it wasn't abuse related, I don't remember if it happened. We rarely talked about anything but the abuse actually. Certainly, this trumped anything I had been previously mad about. What did it really matter if Dawson worked late or forgot to take the garbage out *now*?

Sometimes I felt like those depression ads where the gray cloud hovers over and follows a person. Darkness was always near. I felt like there was nothing worse I could have been told as a parent. In fact our marriage counselor told us this was at the top of the list because even a death would have been more final. This just lingered on forever. And the grief that was destroying me was vast.

At the end of each day, I would drift to sleep. It wasn't like I drifted easily and I was settled. I drifted in pain. I drifted in agony. I was tossing and turning, half awake, listening to Dawson's tossing and turning and sometimes his crying. When I awoke, dried tears would surround my eyes, and my body would ache from all the night's discomfort. The days started slowly.

Once the girls were off to school and Dawson out at work, I couldn't get beyond obsessively dissecting how this had happened. My head would swirl with reviewing the past. *We had therapists for him. Oh, the things I would say to them now.* I could write those scathing letters in my head for hours. "You said you work in the interest of the child, except you missed the depth of his darkness. You MISSed it!" I would yell the letter in my head and then say to myself, *One day I should write this. One day I'll tell her the truth. Oh, and the other therapist—the one who sat me down with Dawson and Sara and explained how I was the root of all Tom's issues. The one who humiliated me saying that I was the reason he was depressed. I was too hard on him; I played favorites with my girls over him. . . . Oh, the volume of the tone I would use to yell at him. And the nutritionist . . . the binge eating. Yes, you are right, it's an eating disorder. Sure! And the school. The tutors. The doctors. Fourteen doctors sat around a table and explained to us after his illness and paralysis that there was a fifty-fifty chance he might actually walk again. Three months in a children's hospital with twenty-four-hour round-the-clock care, and their biggest concern was that the depression meds may not allow him to have an erection.*

I was exhausting myself reliving the conversations over and over. *For crying out loud, he had had help. We knew about his demons, right?* I was endlessly racing through checklists of what "good parents should do" in my head. I was drowning myself in anger, shame, and blame. It was eating me alive. I tore through old pictures, I burned things in the fireplace, I scoured my house clean. I purged his things. I brought a spiritual healer in to renew the house. I did anything to find cleanliness, and yet still I felt no peace. I was ten pounds lighter, uncharacteristically quiet, leaning hard on a second or even a third glass of wine, and my sex life was at long last dead. The one thing that I thought had held us together so far was now gone. I couldn't feel a touch in bed without deeply reliving what had happened to my babies. Every time Dawson would try to reach out, my body would replicate the horror they must have felt. Like a twin that feels her sister's pain, I fought back against touches, sounds, and images as if they were mine. I tried to assure myself I was an adult and my sex life was healthy. I swore to God that I would do anything he wanted. *Just take the pain*, I begged. *Take me! Take my body! You can't have theirs.* But it was too late. The damage was done. *It was donnnnnnne!* And no amount of self-punishment could change this fact. I was fumbling to learn how to pray, and in these moments all I could say was: *Take me—I'll give you anything, Lord! Where are you? Where were you? Why us?* I had to get it together though. I had to find my way out and adjust. This pain needed to be curtailed, of that much I was certain.

After months of pleading and feeling like I just couldn't go on, one night life changed. That night I dropped to bed feeling dead. My brain was fried; my eyes could barely stay open. I couldn't hear one more horrifying story of what had happened under my own roof while I lay in the very bed I was on now. I wanted to die.

Lying there with my eyes slightly open wishing for God to take me, I suddenly felt a warmth in my hands. Next thing I knew I was completely in a zone floating through a tunnel of equal warmth and incredibly bright light. Time seemed to slow. I was afraid I would burn my eyes. Squinting hard to avoid being blinded, I was overwhelmed with trepidation but unable to stop myself from being guided. I told myself over and over again to get my sunglasses from my car, but I never did. I wasn't near my car. Where was I? Nothing seemed to be making sense. Flowing past me like a gentle wind, the light got closer and closer and it saturated me. There were no noises. I had never experienced such silence. Even my thoughts were suspended. A moment passed and the brightness was less intense. It wasn't dark, but I felt immersed in something comforting. My body rested for what seemed like a split second, and I heard a very small voice whisper, *I know I am asking a lot of you.* A wave of oxygen expanded my lungs, and when I released it out, I awoke back in my bed. The weight was gone. The darkness had lifted. Something had changed.

The next day started with a lightness I had never known. I was mad but I wasn't consumed. The rage didn't own me like it once had. People looked different. My memory was the same but cleaner, clearer, less raw. I felt liberated from my own obsessiveness, from the pain, from my sadness, from my own self-torture. It's not that I didn't have any; I just didn't feel chained to it the way I once had. I was open to new endings again. I was free from the unimaginable hate. Unsure of this feeling, I showered, wondering if it would wash away. In the shower I was overcome by water but not shower water. I was flooded in tears, but not my usual tears, either. They were tears of relief. They were clean. At last, freedom from my robotic shell. I went about my day wondering when it would end. Suspicious of what I thought I had been through, I called Joan, now also my spiritual guide. I was still in need of so much help because I had so many doubts. She was a patient friend, and we talked it through. She agreed I was not crazy. Unsure and still needing to know if I was nuts, I began to pray. A lot. If there was a God, I had a long list of questions still and I felt alive enough to ask them.

Renewed with energy, I could feel myself again. I could see Kennedy and Taylor in all their beauty. I didn't die and I embraced that I was going to have to live through this nightmarish experience whether I liked it or not. People kept referring to me as fearless, but I didn't feel resolute in the face of dangers or challenges. I was just alive because my heart was still beating and facing challenges because I had no choice—I had to find resolution within me. It was time for me to pick myself up and be the fearless survivor my girls deserved.

ൟ CHAPTER FIFTEEN

DAWSON'S DAYS WERE LONG. HE ROUTINELY LEFT AROUND 6:00 a.m. and returned close to 8:00 p.m. Any event after work could delay his return until well into the night hours. Certainly, we had started to use some of our therapy-inspired tools. We knew not to interrupt each other, not to judge or assume. We could repeat back what the other had said. But the days were long and for me were filled with triggers, stories, and questions that were painful to work through. I was pretty emotionally spent when he got home. If we were courageous enough to share our days with each other and it didn't end in hard or icky feelings, we considered that a success.

By this time Dawson and I had actually seen a number of therapists. Much like my dating days, some of these experiences were not so good. The first made a full diagnosis for us by saying that I had transition issues, so Dawson was supposed to be sympathetic to my transitions and help me through. Then we saw a therapist who diagnosed dreams—he endlessly evaluated us and somehow never saw the alcoholism in Dawson yet concluded that I had trust issues. This, I believe, is easily diagnosable as I have always been honest about my childhood. I saw a therapist up to and leading into Dawson getting sober. Then Dawson saw a therapist while getting sober. After Dawson's sobriety, we saw a therapist who said that I had anger issues, which seemed pretty explainable to me. *Of course I had anger issues, duh!* She counseled us on how to talk to each other without resentment. I'm not sure I took her up on any of her advice; I had a lot of resentment still. Then we saw a therapist who said that I was too aggressive. She believed that I shouldn't be involved with Tom at all and that Dawson should be able to make his own decisions about money and raising his kid without my consent. Just like dating, I was pretty done with therapists. They seemed ready to listen but more prepared to label and judge.

By the time we got to George, we had heard it all. I felt like they had all pointed the finger at me, and Dawson felt they had all pointed the finger at him. George was different from the start. He gave us three rules: 1. Don't go into the past outside of his room. 2. Divorce talk is off the table. 3. Don't talk about what is said in his office outside that space. We knew therapy all right, but George was going to get us to knowing *us*. He wanted to dive in from day one, our day one. *Honestly,* I thought, *don't we have enough to contend with right where we are? Now we have to go back?* We saw George together once a week, and instead of feeling sorry for us, he put us to challenge after challenge.

While Dawson and I embarked on our individual assignments, the girls did theirs. They were proving to be incredible warriors. They made *everything* into a therapeutic moment. Over the course of our car rides to therapy, we developed an extensive playlist of songs to belt out to reflect whatever mood they were dealing with in that moment: anger, sorrow, excitement. They used stuffed toys that were meant to be emotional conversation tools as a way to discuss hard topics with me. They even used every art supply we had at home to flush out thoughts and feelings. Moreover, they never missed a school day, never turned their anger outward, never ceased to work through their loss and hurt. Coming to terms was first an exercise in shedding their stories. They spoke them, they colored them, and they wrote them. They even dictated to me when their little hands couldn't write as fast as their brains wanted to purge.

Right before we found out about the abuse, Taylor had developed a secret language in which both she and Kennedy could communicate. It was really just English with a British accent. I thought she was imitating my favorite cartoon of theirs, *Peppa Pig*, but it turns out it was a coping mechanism she'd developed to protect herself in the face of danger. It had been a warning sign of how she was shielding their wounded identities and masking their pain and fear.

For as much as Taylor didn't understand fully what had happened, she was determined to overcome whatever obstacles she faced.

She went to school because she had to but hated the transition from home to school, school to daycare, and then back home again. "I don't want to go, Mommy. Can I stay home all day with you? I don't like my teachers, Mommy. Can you pick me up right when the fours class ends?" It was hard to drop her as I didn't like transitions myself. I had to fight the instinct that lay within me to keep them home and guard them with my life. Still, she continued, as we all did, to force herself through the motions of life.

In an effort to take control of my circumstances and, most of all, encourage the possibility of healing, I supplied piles of construction paper and buckets of markers on the floor to color out the wounds and memories. The floor was now a sacred burial ground for drawing memories that we wanted to leave in the past. The second they came home from school, they would grab a snack and set to work. I'll admit these were not drawings for our refrigerator. They were horrifying artistic releases, but they truly helped them work through their confusion. Final pictures often told a story of what had happened in our house. Secrets were revealed on paper that they had been keeping between them and were now an open book for us to see.

"Mommy, look at this." Proudly showing me staircases with stick figures and large stick penises or houses with an x-ed out bedroom where Tom's had once been. As I sat down to discuss the picture, I would struggle to push back the lump in my throat and talk about it as if it was a regular four-year-old drawing. At first, Taylor would start out describing her picture and its details, and soon Kennedy would interrupt to complete the image. They had collective information that bonded them in a unique way. Over time, the art became so helpful that they began three-ring binders for themselves, and the activities started to teach them both reading and writing skills. They also began taking their stories to the therapists' offices each week, and that only intensified their progress.

KENNEDY WAS IN our local elementary public school when we discovered what Tom had done. It was a safe place for her; he had never attended there, leaving no memories for her in that space. In the early days, things unfolded at a rapid pace, and I needed to address the issue with the principal almost immediately. Crisis changes a child's behavior, and I wanted Kennedy to be understood. I had no plan. There was no playbook for that kind of conversation, no advice blog on how to handle it or who to tell. In fact, when I showed up with no appointment and asked for the principal, I reassured myself—I thought *she* would be okay based on my first impression of her. The girls and I had met her briefly before school started. This was her first year. At that point we had introduced ourselves, and our big story at the time was a recovering handicapped brother and the recent passing of our beloved dog. She was incredibly interested and kind. Here I was preparing for a very different kind of conference and thinking, *Oh God, give me the words to tell her what I need to say.*

I asked somewhat frantically if she was around, and the consistently emotionless secretary barely looked up when she said, "Besty isn't here. You can try Paul in his office around the corner."

Shit! I thought. There is not a *she*—only a *he*, and I didn't want to face a *he* right now. Still, my adrenaline was flowing, and I felt compelled to charge forward. My courage was surging *now*. I would not be deterred.

I rounded the corner, never having stepped foot in his office before or even having met him, for that matter. My heart raced, my head spun as I considered what I should say.

I barged in, skipping the small talk, and sat myself down just as the lump hit my throat hard and big. I took a deep breath, filling my lungs, and began to talk. The anxiety relieved my brain of its ability to think, and as if I had just finished a marathon, I was struggling for air. I blurted out who I was and who my daughter was. While I was speaking quickly, my voice shook. I was still gasping for air but didn't want to stop myself to take a breath for fear that the words would be replaced by tears. I continued that Kennedy had been sexually abused by her half brother and I just needed to update the school that she was in trauma. *There!* It was short and quick, but I was done. I looked up from my ashamed position, hands shaking, the lump in my throat becoming even bigger. The elephant-size tears started; *crap, tears are in his eyes too!* The truth is that though I had married a man who cried, seeing it as a direct result of my unveiling, in a stranger no less, was different. On this topic, I had become comfortable when a woman cried but a man, *UGH! I was not prepared. This situation is really bad.* No matter how much I knew it was bad in my heart, nothing reminded me more than another person's reaction, which full-force said, *WOW, this is really bad!* It was humbling, and yet it was our life. This wasn't the last time I would make a man cry with this story. And not the last time that the numbness lended by our daily routine would be peeled away, reminding me that this *was* a horrific crime.

I looked back down and in horror realized I was still in pajama pants.

IT TOOK ABOUT a week and more tearful meetings for the teachers and administrators to rally themselves into a safety net for us. With our permission, the school worked closely with the outside therapists, and we all worked together like an all-American team.

There is no 504 or IEP that covers trauma-related learning gaps, but the school developed an emergency plan anyway. There were point people in place for Kennedy during any part of her day if something triggered her memories or made her uncomfortable. The principal, the assistant principal, the school psychologist, the teachers, and the nurse were all on call if something came up. And it did.

A kiss from a kindergarten boy, a shove in the lunch line, a gooey food, anything that may have seemed harmless and regular in a typical child's day could send Kennedy into a total meltdown. I was sure to get an update after it was over.

ON THE OUTSIDE, the girls were appropriately growing and connecting, but like our world, theirs was small too. Two days a week their time was reserved for therapy. Their friends were out playing soccer or doing gymnastics, and they spent ten to thirty minutes in the car, depending on the day, for each of them to have a one-hour appointment. All told we could spend three hours detained, if I didn't add extra time by talking with the therapist myself or if we weren't stuck in highway traffic. We had each other though.

In the car we had one rule—you could sing, as long as you tried to sing in tune. So we sang. Anything from Adele to Billy Joel, Blake Shelton, Taylor Swift, James Taylor—you name it. If we liked the song, we downloaded it to my phone and belted it out together. Songs that brought tears, songs that released anger—songs that ignited all three of us in three different ways at the same time. And when the music would soften one of the girls enough, it often informed a conversation. Driving down the road, I had to do a lot of explaining. True there were times to laugh about the talks, like the time Justin Timberlake's "Sexy Back" came on and the girls were fighting about whether the word in the song was *sex* or *sexy*. That might have been a hilarious viral You-Tube video had it not been so personal. I had to explain that it was in fact both words and then explain what they both meant.

As much fun as the singing provided, there were also moments of seriousness in the car. Often they asked me questions that no mom should have to answer: "Mom, did your brother do this to you?" or "Mom, is it supposed to hurt?" I tried to cry silently, but sometimes a sniffle would call me out. One time, I was weeping and Kennedy asked me, "Mommy, will you ever stop crying?" To which I answered that it's a parent's job to protect their kids and I was very sad about what had happened. To which Kennedy responded, "Well, you screwed that up!" We all broke into laughter, and I quickly defended myself by asserting that once I knew, it had ended, but the fact that in spite of everything she could maintain her sense of humor encouraged me to keep my own.

Each laugh helped to stamp out the sad memories. And each new memory replaced a bad memory. Our new life was growing on us and it was comforting. We were creating building blocks where there was once only rubble. Between Dawson and I, the smaller gestures were growing: a hug or a handhold, a seedling of connection again. Hard conversations only got easier when we worked hard to listen. We had to dial back our desires to feel heard or defend our sides. Then sometimes we needed space to just speak and not have each other respond. Listening was a test of patience almost nightly. Sometimes we were better than others. I needed Dawson to understand how I felt, a mother raising two tiny abuse survivors. I needed a hug and tenderness in my own pain and loss. I needed him to wipe my tears with empathy as I poured out my fears. But he couldn't consistently be that person. My fears were daggers of reminder to him of what his son had done to his daughters. He needed my forgiveness and understanding so that he could help Tom grow into a better person too. He needed me to see a father torn, and so, often I couldn't be that person for him either. I wanted to compartmentalize Tom out of my world and that wasn't an option for Dawson.

All the same, we kept working to stay connected and, if we needed to, reconnect. The first Christmas as we were driving away from George's office, after a particularly hard but honest session, he proclaimed to me that he had never felt closer. With his hand on my knee, stopping for a particularly long time at a stop sign, he leaned in for a warm and loving kiss so much like our first kiss, my heart skipped a beat.

Feeling optimistic after that day's breakthrough, I looked forward to the Christmas season with nearly the same amount of excitement and glow as had been my habit for years. I love the lights decorating the streets and neighborhoods. I love the extra kindness people display. I love the smells of pine, orange, vanilla, and cookies. I love the sounds of pine needles quietly dropping from the tree, music in every store, and children laughing. The day after Thanksgiving I start a very comprehensive Christmas playlist that is constantly playing in the car and throughout the house. It plays right through until New Year's Day. I love gathering the last thoughtful things for everyone on my list. I even spend a week or two thinking of who will get a special Santa gift from me. And once my heart tells me who in my life needs a little pick-me-up, I happily deliver it without a word to anyone.

The warmth radiates from me at Christmas, and I was energized by hope that year, and unwilling to let anything get in the way of "my time." If there was no call from the girls' school or from Utah, it was just a routine day and that was a welcome blessing. I continued to remind myself that the abuse was over and the bubbling cauldron that had once been brewing was no longer in our lives. Slow days, family time, and getting to know each other again were turning out to be really fun.

BEFORE WE KNEW it, February had come, and we were heading on a much-needed vacation. Dawson and I had been married on the west coast of Florida. We hadn't planned on having a wedding party, actually, just a ceremony, but that didn't fly with my sister and father. Instead we ended up having a small wedding with a justice of the peace at a Hyatt Resort. After that, it had become a special place because I also had a childhood friend who lived nearby. It was a nice spot to return to every year for those two reasons. Over time the girls had come to love it for their own reasons—like the lazy river and the eight pools. Unfortunately, as therapy for the girls had unfolded that first winter, we soon discovered our sacred hideout was also where the abuse had started. Since we had paid for it for already, we embraced it as an opportunity to face the reality head-on. Dawson was pretty calm about it; I was terrified it would bring up a lot of bad feelings for the girls. The best I could wish for was a new beginning, but I was filled with nerves and anxiety and using the old unhelpful strategy of projecting the what-ifs.

At home, we were surrounded in secrets, and we needed to relax. I needed to let loose, feel free from the dark cloud, and experience a colorful Florida sky. We happily replaced the cold northeastern days and winter clothes with bare feet in the sand and warm days and nights. Upon arriving, we went straight to the tiny, grassy, golf course–like green in the rear of the hotel. There was a large pond that had an even larger fountain. We had planned to have communion and a prayer on that site, which was where I had walked down the hotel yard in flowing, breezy white to take Dawson's hand in marriage. I had brought a gypsy-type blanket that we laid out in the field. The sun was setting over the pond, and we were all glad to be off a plane and in a new environment away from the claustrophobia we felt back home. I had packed matzo crackers and a little Welch's grape juice. We sat in a circle in plain view and held hands as we prayed for new beginnings. We each took a piece of cracker. Taylor actually required an entire cracker, needing a little bit more than symbolic bread for her hunger. We sipped the grape juice after a toast, and we reveled in our relief over the few days of peace ahead.

Despite all my worries, it was easy to float away for the next seven days, simply basking in the sun and warmth. We even took part in the miracle of a baby bald eagle flying for the first time, from a nest we had seen being built the year prior.

A bald eagle nest is an estimated five feet around. It is used year after year because it takes them so long and requires so much effort to make. Some can be as large as nine feet around. Bald eagles mate for life, and unlike most animals in the wild, the mother and father eagles will raise and protect their eaglets together. Approximately 40 percent of eaglets die, however, in their first attempt at flight.

To me this seemed like a sign. So I googled *eagles in the Bible* and what they meant in that context. I had begun to find so much comfort in my faith that I was constantly searching for God in any way possible and sought signs bigger and broader than the wind. I wanted to see and hear every message that could be given. The eagle is a symbol of those nations whom God employs and sends forth to do a work of destruction, sweeping away whatever is decaying. I didn't know what any of that might mean for us. All I knew was that here we were, at the site in which we began our relationship, witnessing a couple bound together through potential tragedy and sticking together no matter what. Something was destroyed, but something new was beginning.

CHAPTER SIXTEEN

FILLED WITH RENEWED ENERGY AND HOPE, WE RETURNED home thinking that it was time to put the house up for sale. We had incredibly mixed feelings about doing so because of our happy memories here and the hard work we had done in recovery in this space. At one point we discussed moving from town all together, but we were in the midst of an incredible turn of events. We thought the change to a new house would sustain this renewed feeling.

Our hearts were beginning to feel rest now that we were hearing less and less new information, so we had begun to live our lives again. Statistics vary, but most sources say that one out of every three women will be victims of sexual assault in her lifetime, some 60 percent before the age of eighteen. Over 90 percent of those children and young women will know their attacker, and because of that less than 12 percent will attempt to tell until it's too late. As Dawson and I had started to realize, those statistics were all too true. One by one, as we needed to tell various people our story, women came forward and told us that it was their story too. In fact, the number of women who revealed their pasts to us became a source of great bonding. In those touching moments I took on a great responsibility to be the mom who believed, and fostered strength and love. More times than I can count, women thanked me for trusting Kennedy and Taylor. Something in our belief offered healing to them as well.

It was a few weeks before Easter, and Taylor was turning four. We cleaned up the house, freshening paint, sorting through our excess stuff. We cleaned and purged. We donated or threw out all of Tom's things. His Legos were shipped to my sister; his bed was sent to the dump. We turned his room into an office for Dawson. We changed the girls' comforters and bedroom decor. Then we listed the house for sale.

A week or two went by and we were antsy that the house wasn't selling, so my friend offered to bring us a statue of Saint Joseph, the patron saint of real estate, to bury in the yard. I accepted it. Dawson was in Vegas when it arrived. In the pouring rain I determinedly buried him according to the directions. I said a lengthy prayer and placed him upside down, facing the house in his plastic bag. It was lonely burying him and praying for the next steps, but a wave of right-seeming words came over me, and I felt in good hands with my faith. I was the agent on our house, so there wasn't anyone to even share this news with. In anticipation, I went to bed.

The next day, I went through a routine morning. Another day of rain and the yard was mud. I became drenched just getting the girls in the car and off to school. Sure, gardens were lush, but we couldn't even enjoy them because it was too wet! Upon my return home, I was drawn back to my saint in the garden for no particular reason. Instead of covering my head to avoid the rain and heading in to the house, I took a few steps toward where I had buried him the night before. To my surprise, there he was. The dirt was in fact in a neat pile where I had temporarily put it to dig my hole. The saint was in a clean and unharmed bag, out of the hole and to the left. Conventional wisdom would say that an animal had dug him up, but there were no evident bite or paw marks. The bag was just as clean as it was when I had first buried it. *But he had been buried deep in the mud, and it was still raining—how was the bag clean? Too weird!* It was just the saint lying there as if I had never quite finished putting him deep in the ground.

In a completely perplexed state, I called Dawson immediately to discuss the strange scenario. Trying not to cast judgment on my recounting of the events, we talked it through. We agreed that this was a sign and that maybe God had different plans for us. That day we took the house off the market. After all, Easter was upon us and a saint had just unearthed itself in our yard.

THE MORE COMFORTABLE I became in my faith, the more I had come to love Easter. It seemed like a newer new year to me than New Year's itself. The idea that Jesus died and was resurrected wasn't something I spent time overthinking though. That was heady stuff and hard to relate to. I simplified it for myself and the girls—people were afraid, they did a bad thing as a result of that fear, and yet something really amazing happened in the end. We hunkered down that year, living only one day at a time. The girls were involved in sports and school, and were, for the most part, happy, and so slowly their brains had begun to be free and clean again. They continued to progress in their learning, and despite the insurmountable cost of the tragedy financially, Dawson's new job was a blessing at just the right time. Although he was working long hours, he also found the time he needed for court and family obligations. He helped us get back on track financially. We were no longer in debt and actually starting to save at a rapid pace. Things were undeniably starting fresh for us. A bad thing had happened and we had been terribly afraid, but here we were, embarking on a new chapter.

Forgiveness is a matter of letting go of the pain. It has been a daily choice for me and a daily struggle. In the beginning, the rage scorched me. After a while, time created a distance that soothed my heart and that my mind craved. I was trapped though—no matter how much I wanted to let go of Tom, if I stayed married to Dawson, he was still part of my family. He would still always be Kennedy and Taylor's half brother. It was never lost on me. The only way out was through, together. Dawson clung to the hope that I could one day forgive him, often telling me that was what got him out of bed in the morning. I took solace in the signs all around me, most especially the wind. *Why did this all happen?* I never stopped asking and neither did the girls, but I still had no answers. It was a humbling reminder that I didn't know everything.

Kennedy turned six right as the leaves began to turn colors again. The fall brought mixed feelings for us. The therapists said it would often be a reminder of the turmoil we endured during that fall of 2011. October 2012 was definitely shadowed for me, since it was the first year. The girls were just in crappy moods but weren't sure why. They weren't fussy kids normally, but those Octobers brought about certain emotional imbalances, trouble sleeping, and usually a meltdown or two about something uncontrollable like growing out of a favorite pair of pajamas.

Again, though, the passing of time felt like a blessing as we charged toward Christmas once again. On played the carols, my energy lifted, the kitchen was buzzing, the house was decorated, the mistletoe was hanging, and Christmas miracles were in the air.

Yes, Tom weighed heavily between us still. Maybe he always would. I could not share Dawson's hope for his recovery from his heinous acts, and my heart was no longer with him as a child of mine. It was different for Dawson; he was torn up about three children in pain. For better or worse, Tom was Dawson's son. The only thing I could offer our marriage was granting Dawson that if Tom did recover, that was ultimately best for Kennedy and Taylor, therefore investing in his rehabilitation was the best solution. I dug deep in wanting Kennedy and Taylor to one day be proud of our decisions. I wanted to be able to face them when they asked us the deeper questions themselves. And I wanted them to be able to put this behind them and see that Tom had a chance because of their courage and honesty. Often this wasn't quite enough for our marriage, but it was all I had to give.

Maintaining a calm presence when decisions rolled around was for the most part a brutal task for me. In light of new information, whatever it was, I would instantly feel my heart beating faster and my hands start to shake with anxiety and fear, and in spite of my best efforts, sometimes my anger won the day. In one moment I could be calm, and in the next I was fuming with rage. I had to learn to ground myself or my feelings clouded my thinking. I was not always good at that, however, and my failings led to arguments with Dawson. No one benefitted from the times I let my anger arrest me. Therapists suggested that writing a journal would help, but I resisted, believing that in writing, it was all too real. On one particularly angry day, I felt consumed by it, so I wrote a letter to Tom's mother. Now, she had always made me uncomfortable, but I had never exploded on her the way I'd *wanted* to. Now I wrapped up years' worth of fury and unleashed it in writing.

Dear Sara,

Suffice it to say that I am glad this year is ending. And with that I am going to do something I have wanted to do for a long time. . . .

And from there I let go of every bit of anger I had ever had at that woman. It ended with:

Now that I have gotten a few things off my chest, I am good.
[No signature.]

It didn't change a thing between us, but it did offer me yet another incentive to start using that pediatric dose of Xanax various people kept suggesting I use.

Then there was the time in court when the prosecuting attorney who was representing the girls, who was determined to divide Dawson and me, couldn't get it straight that Tom was a half brother. Each court date, Sara and Tom sat to the right of the judge along with Tom's attorney. Dawson and I sat to the left of the judge behind the prosecuting attorney. She would stand up and introduce the case and each time call Tom the stepbrother of the victims. After a few court dates, it really began to bother me that she didn't know her clients. So even with my tiny medical dose of help in me, one day I popped up, interrupted the court, and quite loudly corrected her that he was a *HALF* brother. The judge—a calm, older, seasoned man—said, "Mrs. Miller, this is not a TV courtroom. If you cannot stay quiet, we will have to remove you."

It was true: I needed to stick to the meditation my minister charged me with each morning. These types of explosions weren't good for anyone, and didn't bring me any real peace. Meditation helped me to refocus my thoughts and sometimes even silence my brain. It was hard to stay focused on the long-term good of this situation. I needed the centering, and I needed to apply the positive strategies of coping that I was pressing my girls to use. I worked harder to spend the daily ten minutes or so soothing my mind and appreciating the silence.

EVEN THOUGH MY outbursts disrupted my peace rounding out 2012, I was looking forward to 2013. I have always joked that odd years were better years for me. And this particular odd year I was turning forty. I have also always believed that I was *born* forty. So I had been teasing for a while that I was finally going to be my "real" age.

On New Year's Eve, the girls and I sat by the fire playing another torturous round of Go Fish with *Finding Nemo* cards. Man, I hated that game! But we laughed anyway because Taylor couldn't pronounce any of the cards she was asking for. I still felt the emptiness on the ground where Morgan had worn the varnish off the floor, but still we laughed and had fun as the flames crackled and we discussed our New Year's goal.

It had been four years now since we had started the Family Goal wall. Actually, it had started when Tom had had so many physical therapy goals that we decided to support him by making goals of our own; that way he wouldn't be singled out.

Back then, as a part of physical therapy, the hospital had suggested that Tom add swim therapy to his routine. They didn't have a pool, however, so they gave me the exercises, and Tom and I set out again to be pool partners. Each week we would go to the Y, where I had special permission for him to do his therapeutic work during the adult swim hours. Soon enough he was back on the team. One day they had a guest speaker come and talk to them about the importance of goals. He brought home a sheet that was handed out, and I decided we should *all* have goals. I typed out the definition of *goal*: the end to which all effort is directed. The first step to achieving your goal is to share it, so in that first year (and each year after) I cut out twenty or so badly shaped ovals from construction paper. Everyone had to define a goal, set its completion time, and add any other important information. It was a source of family support and togetherness. Even Morgan had had a goal or two in her day.

So as we sat that night by the warm glow of the fire, we came up with some ideas for our wall, which neither of the girls wanted to let go. They suggested we celebrate the new year with something pertaining to the number thirteen. They realized I was turning forty in a thirteen year and that thirteen was my lucky number. I loved this idea. But what? We were ready for a refreshing year, and as we sat there thinking, we missed Dawson who was still at the office with his not-into-the-holidays boss. We called him. He was quick to add to our germ of an idea. "Let's do a family celebration on the thirteenth of every month." We had a collective end to which all our efforts would be directed. Our mission was set.

A NEW YEAR was beginning. I loved the laughing fits we found ourselves in. Connected pinkies were becoming connected lips. Hugging and kissing were back in our house more than ever before. Conversations were still deep but more lively, and fewer ended in tears.

One afternoon during a mundane therapy activity, I was putting together a picture project and a short biography of the girls' lives before, during, and after the abuse for therapy. It was to help the therapist work with each one of them to retrain their brains out of post-traumatic stress syndrome. In this exercise you go back to the points of trauma and teach your brain that the action was bad, but you are not bad. It's a therapeutic practice that is starting to have excellent results for kids who have less baggage to unpack in sessions. I asked Kennedy if she could recall a time that was loving before all the bad stuff happened. "Mommy," she said, "we didn't have love in our house before. We do now." It was true that our whole outlook on life had changed, and love now had a whole new meaning. Her simple commentary resonated—the love we were building had consistency and intention, and provided a sense of belonging. I had spent the better part of my life feeling misunderstood. It is probably the most hurtful element of my life. I deeply wanted to belong everywhere I had been in my almost forty years. In this new tiny little world we had created, there was deep understanding among us even when we weren't in agreement. We presented our most authentic, vulnerable selves at home and slowly we had strength and belonging because of it.

My energy from Christmas flowed right into January, when every trip to the grocery store gave us an excuse to an-alyze the ice cream aisle. Our first Thirteenth Party would be a tasting of thirteen kinds of ice cream. It was pretty exciting. The individual serving sizes now sold in the stores made the tasting less intimidating, but it was hard to choose which thirteen ice creams would make the cut.

When we finally arrived at the thirteenth of January, we were all eagerly anticipating the experience. The four of us eagerly sat at the edge of the counter that only comfortably fits one. As we huddled there together with taste buds ready, our energy mounted as the top of the first sample was removed by Dawson. The little pop when it released its seal gave us the go sign to lift our spoons and fight for the first scoop. We gave one another details about how much or little our tongues appreciated any given bite. It was simple, the deepness of the chocolate, or the smoothness of the vanilla flavoring. Even the different types of crunch that were achieved by a nut or a chip, we analyzed each delicious spoonful. Taylor complained of a brain freeze, and we all shivered a bit thinking of it. We savored each bite with mouths watering for the next. It was great practice for us. Keeping it simple, delighting in the moment, and just leaning in to the sweetness of the connection. Our laughter filled the kitchen air. The room was warm with genuine gestures, and time stood still as four hearts settled on the perfect flavors and combination with each answer being the right one.

We were afloat in ideas for what to do for the rest of the months of the year. In February we did an artistic project to express our gratitude and love for thirteen family members or friends. We set to work on the floor, which expanded our workspace beyond what any of our tables could offer. Kennedy pulled out the large bin of crayons, markers, colored pencils, and even chalk from the craft closet and set to planning our work. We traced our hands left and right, close to each other, then traced smaller hands slightly over the top, and even smaller hands slightly over those, and added a trunk to make a tree. The blank white piece of printer paper was slowly transformed by an outline in pencil. Eventually a tree in bloom emerged, and finally it was colored with any combination of the rainbow the girls chose. The floor became cluttered with rolling and spreading supplies as we worked on each of the thirteen different trees.

"Where is the white crayon?"

"What is Aunt Lisa's favorite color?"

"Are we mailing one to Grandma?"

We hummed for hours customizing each note. Crafting filled our thoughts with kindness, and the joy consumed us just as it consumed every square inch of the kitchen floor. On February 14 each of the letters were mailed with our intent to spread our love.

Each laughing and bonding session added to our shield of armor. It reminded me how fearless we were becoming. Fearless doesn't mean there is nothing to fear though, and Kennedy and Taylor had their fears. From the outside they looked like they had the perfect friendship. In fact, parents from our social circle often remarked that the girls always got along and never fought. I usually shrugged my shoulders and let their comments linger out there. The whole picture is that they really did get along and they really were good friends, but they had been through an awful lot together. Privately there was more to it, and people didn't need to know the details. Doctors and researchers have studied the bonding that happens through tragedy. It can go both ways—people can bond together or break apart. My girls were no exception.

They had to deal with both the bonding and the breaking in their own ways. Kennedy and Taylor needed to reestablish boundaries. They needed to reestablish their own body space. They needed to reestablish trust. And while the immediate physical fear was gone, routine parts of life could provoke a subconscious sense of fear that their brain had to learn to control. The naked splash of a joint sisterly bath could trigger a reaction. The close proximity of a warm body while sleeping made sleeping in the same bed a fistfight. They often struggled to differentiate their feelings from one another. "Mommy, I had a bad day at school today," would often be followed with "Can we talk in private?" And yet, they still cared deeply for each other in spite of these lasting effects. They would bounce home after school, chatting away about their days to each other like they didn't have a care in the world.

"Oh, I did that in kindergarten. Did you do the slime project?" "How was your gym class? Did you play four square?"

Their conversation usually lasted up until they realized they were hungry or until I said, "Uh-hum, hi, my name is Mommy . . . anyone want to tell me how their day was?"

They also worked hard to understand Dawson's relationship with his son. Asking questions like:

"Does he still love Tom like he loves us?" "Will he leave us to take care of Tom?"

They were left with an insecure feeling in their hearts every time Dawson left for a business trip, wondering if he would return. All of those same insecurities were worse when we fought. On top of those things, I expected a lot from them, I held them to a high standard of behavior. Once told by an expert that hurt kids, *hurt* kids—I wasn't going to let the girls become the playground bully.

Two other mothers and I put together a foursome tennis lesson for the girls that spring. When one of the mothers went to go pick up all four girls at the end of the lesson, she reported back to me that she had had to pull Taylor off of Kennedy, who she had tackled. As she said this, my face grew white with horror at their poor choices, but Heather was laughing. In fact, as I was apologizing for their bad behavior and looking for them to make them apologize as well, she stopped me and said, "I loved it." Taken aback a bit, I gave her a funny face. "I loved it," she repeated. "Your girls never fight. It made me happy to see them disagree." At the end of the day, they were just close sisters. Sisters who had been through extraordinary circumstances together. Sisters who needed to separate themselves in some ways for their own sanity. And sisters who occasionally tackled each other at tennis, proving their normality, which was progress that I needed to welcome.

Each idea the girls had for a monthly Thirteenth Party really represented who they were. Kennedy always came up with very grand and elaborate plans. Taylor's ideas were straightforward and simple. Knowing this about them empowered me as a mom. It helped me guide and direct their future childhood experiences. In the same way that their party ideas reflected their natures, their methods while doing the projects helped me learn about them. I had always known that Kennedy was a perfectionist at heart and held herself up to standards as high as mine. Soon it became clear to me that Taylor would do everything upside down and backward before she would acquiesce to completing the task in a conventional way. March became another opportunity to watch and discover how my girls learned, because we were going to attempt to do thirteen puzzles in one night. We had puzzles of all sizes ranging from 20 to 150 pieces. Some were twelve-feet long with large pieces, and some were the usual rectangle with smaller pieces, each having their own themes. We all chose a puzzle and jumped right into our own zone, both mentally and physically. Kennedy worked piecing together each by shape and size, looking for the right shape to fill each hole. Taylor made connections by color, able to associate the slight shade change from one piece to another in amazingly subtle ways. Bent over on our hands and knees staring at the floor, we sorted through the piles of cardboard that would eventually form each picture. The room was quiet and filled with concentration until one of us would mumble, "Ah, I thought I had it!" or "YES, I found the piece I wanted!" Side by side working toward a collective achievement, the minutes and hours passed, revealing thirteen colorful images and ob-scuring the tan carpet below.

My knees were burning with pain from being on the floor for so long. Achy and stiff from being on all fours, our bones cracked and muscles snapped as we rose and stretched. The glorious sight of the entire floor filled with the constructed puzzles was worth our creakiness. And the reflection of our patient, thoughtful, hard work one step at a time was a metaphor of our life constructed, deconstructed, and recon-structed.

The monthly family events gave us unity around some-thing besides abuse talk. I cherished the gift of this change. We always carved out time to talk about our feelings and still used music, art, and other forms of therapy to process what we were going through, but the Thirteenth Parties, as we called them, shifted the conversation in a different direction.

"Remember the time we couldn't find that last piece of the Snoopy puzzle?"

"Can we do that puzzle again?"

"Remember the chocolate-chip peanut-butter flavor Chips Ahoy things? Can you buy more of them?"

"Maybe there is a new flavor at the store, let's check."

"Dad, Dad, Dad, I have an idea for a Thirteenth Party. . . ."

And on it went.

In April we finally got off the floor and took to the kitchen, crafting a very special birthday cake. My mother had become increasingly helpful with the kids. She was the best grandmother, solidly involved in their interests and lives. As an expert at homework and projects, she helped them work through any school issues. Often on the sidelines admonishing me for cheering too loudly, my mom was a regular. The girls had become very fond of doing special things for her, and this year of all years her birthday landed on Friday the thirteenth. Having heard just enough school talk about how spooky Friday the thirteenth was, the girls were very excited to celebrate Grandma's birthday that day for our special event. Instead of scary surprises, we savored freshly made vanilla cake slathered with smooth and rich-tasting vanilla buttercream that had been molded into a book, representing Grandma's favorite thing: reading. Our mouths watered for each forkful of goodness. We finished the night full in our hearts and stomachs.

Toward the end of 2012, the longing for a new four-legged pet had overcome us. Dawson and I talked at length about getting a puppy. We feared getting another unhealthy Berner like Morgan. Emotionally we were attached to the breed though. So one of my coworkers helped us find a

Bernese mountain dog breeder. She gave me the name of a woman in Canada. When I looked her up, her website page was the same exact layout as my agent page. I took it as a sign to contact her right away. We immediately bought the one female left for purchase.

When the big weekend came to go get the dog, however, no amount of excitement could mask the tension between Dawson and me. We began the drive to Canada in a pretty dark place. Working with George, our final therapist, had shed light on a lot of unavoidable and uncomfortable truths. In the beginning, George sorted through all the other therapists' theories on our problems and rarely spent time talking about the immediate issues, although he was always eager to hear how the girls and Tom were doing. And while Dawson and I took the rules he laid out quite seriously, the icky feelings from some sessions lingered long after the one hour in his office. This was one of those times.

We left my mom with the girls for the night. Sitting down for what would be a ten-hour drive to Canada, we were silent. The goal was to pick up a ten-week-old Bernese mountain dog and arrive home on May thirteenth to surprise the girls, but our adventure started out with a disagreement and a blame fest.

With my knees turned to the passenger-side window and my nose running, I stubbornly let my silent tears fall. I'm not even sure what had me so worked up. But I was mad, and if there was anything that infuriated Dawson, it was being trapped in a car with me crying, knowing he was unable to fix it.

To pass the time as my emotions brewed, I quietly demanded answers in prayer: "Well, God, if you exist, show me . . ." I challenged him to show me the number thirteen along the road. Within a mile of our driveway a thirteen quickly revealed itself. *Too easy*, I thought. So I looked for another and another. Thirteens were now coming faster and faster. In fact, the whole thirteenth mile of a highway was marked every tenth of a mile. Was this God's way of laughing at me? By the time we got to the breeder's tiny two-bedroom cottage, I had seen more than seventy-six thirteens, and after each one, I was a bit softened. We hadn't solved anything upon arrival. I was willing to let it go though.

THE LITTER WAS six pups: Red, Orange, Yellow, Green, Blue, and Purple; easy pup names to keep track of for a breeder, but they'd soon be changed by their new owners. To me, however, the rainbow was a sign of God's promise to Noah that the rain was over and good things would come in our life. At the door we were greeted by Yellow, who came bounding over, stumbling with her giant paws, sliding the rest of the way on the wood floor until she came to a complete four-paws-out stop! It was settled; we were back on the road with a twenty-five-pound puppy, filled with spunk and personality, that looked like a fuzzy bear cub. Her new name was Tahoe. Exhausted, we arrived home to two ecstatic girls on May thirteenth, just as planned.

THE GIRLS STILL went to therapy every week. We had stopped seeing the trauma therapist, Jill, however, because she was so far away and that therapy had run its course. Now we had Nancy. She had gentle, wise, grandmotherly qualities, especially the gray hair always tied back in a bun. She spoke softly and slowly. Every hurtful story flowed like soothing poetry from her mouth even though it wasn't poetic. She could repeat horrific things to me and to Dawson without eliciting any defensiveness. I ran almost every decision and every motherly process through Nancy. Nancy nurtured my soul, which was wired to second-guess a lot in the beginning. Nancy pushed me down paths I was afraid of walking. Nancy retired and in retirement still saw the girls. When she didn't have an office space, she would even come to our house for family meetings and fight mitigation. Nancy was, as she once said, a part of our team.

Nancy challenged us to proactively teach new body rules and appropriate boundaries. She would say: Pinch their bottoms, squeeze their arms and legs, snuggle them so they don't fear what a good touch is. Host every playdate, monitor their interactions. See how they play with others. Dawson, you are the most important male figure they will have; you will shape the way they see men forever.

In family meetings Nancy allowed the girls to ask their questions to Dawson—"Daddy, do you want to leave us and take care of Tom?"—and then waited for Dawson to reassure them, reiterating his words, making them more real. Nancy often checked in with just Dawson and me as well and pressed us to be committed, knowing that together we were stronger and so the girls would be.

I had given up therapy at this point and replaced it with prayer and a spiritual advisor. Dawson had never really loved any one therapist, so he ultimately settled on a spiritual advisor as well. We wanted to move on, and rehashing had become tiring. Even our trusted George visits were beginning to feel forced, and we only saw him for another six months. For all of us, it had just gotten old walking into doctor's offices, sitting in waiting rooms, explaining our wounds, and coming out pretending that our hearts were not just in surgery.

JUNE WAS DAWSON'S birthday. He didn't grow up celebrating his birthday, so we always enjoyed spoiling him against his will. We decided on a scavenger hunt for our Thirteenth Party. It just worked out that Dawson was on a business trip over his birthday, the eleventh, and would return home on the thirteenth. So I set about creating the hunt, which included thirteen clues to ultimately set up and decorate for the party. The girls each had one friend joining us. The four of them filled the house with their giggles and high-pitched, young voices, as they excitedly anticipated the adventure.

"Wait, the next clue is in the mailbox. . . . We have to check the mailbox." Then the click of the front door, followed by its slam as they went off, and momentarily the house was quiet.

"Get the marker bin, we have to make a poster. Where is the paper?" Pounding footsteps followed by the thump and scratch of puppy paws whizzing through the kitchen to get the appropriate supplies. The smell of the kitchen got richer and deeper as I happily made dinner and spruced up the house for Dawson's return, while each clue was solved. It was the first time we had let anyone in on our special celebrations, and it was fun having some new insiders join the adventure.

CHAPTER SEVENTEEN

FAITH AND FOREGIVENESS SOMETIMES FELT LIKE A JACKET that didn't fit and no amount of pulling or tugging made it more comfortable, but I was stuck in it and needed to make it work. I spent hours waffling back and forth about it. Conventionally, forgiveness means to stop feeling anger toward someone who has done something wrong to you, to stop blaming them or requiring payment. But forgiveness is also widely thought of as a pardon or a mercy—maybe even an absolution—something I couldn't give. One Christian-based website suggested that to forgive was to "wipe the slate clean." Whose slate, mine or theirs? Now that my head was slightly above water and happiness was returning in tiny glimmers, these were thoughts that rented a little bit of my brain space. Can one really "wipe the slate clean" after being trapped, held down, and misused? How do you pardon someone who has murdered another person's boundaries and crushed their control over the one thing in life that is truly theirs—their own bodies? Often I tried to close my eyes and envision it happening to me so that I could take it away from the girls. As if in my head I could erase their experience and take the pain. I couldn't.

As we navigated our way through the *un*justice system, as I'd come to think of it, I was frequently told to prepare myself for everyone to lose, meaning no matter the solution there was no punishment that could make good on the crime. Unlike other crimes, there is no "pass" on your first abuse. That crime is finite, like murder; there is no way to *learn* to do better. Yes, you can go on to never commit that crime again, but it happened to the victim and they can't erase it or wipe *their* slate clean. My sticking point was that I had to consider that the guilty verdict would condemn this thirteen-year-old for life. And not just any thirteen-year-old, but my husband's son. Frequently forced to confront these questions was torture, and I knew there was no real answer. Even in the judge's final statement he said, "Son, you are the only person in this room who will walk out with a clean slate in the public eye, but son, I want you to know there will always be someone in your life you can overpower. And you will have to work to control yourself forever. Son, you have unleashed a 'lion' in yourself. Now I don't want you to hear 'cat.' I want you to hear 'lion.'" The words were sobering. Tom was the only one who could walk through life unmarked by what he had done; there would never be a time for him to sit down with his girlfriend or wife and say, "Honey, I love you and I need to tell you something about me." Unlike the girls who would one day find the man they wanted to marry and sit him down to say, "Honey, I love you and you need to know something about me. . . ." As a juvenile, Tom's record would be sealed, and he would get to start his life over if he chose to with only his conscience to accuse him. The girls, on the other hand, were now distinctly different, with a life that would include forever avoiding the shadow of an unwanted body in their memory and space.

Tom spent about two weeks in juvenile detention before he was released back to his mother's. There he was free until he was moved to Utah. During that time he saw a judge twice.

His case was settled in about two years. We had three judges during that time and two different probation officers. We were told our case was incredibly speedy. Pleading guilty meant everything was prenegotiated. With much trepidation between Dawson and me, to plead guilty meant validation for the girls and lesser charges for Tom, along with avoiding jail.

Over those two-plus years, though, Dawson, Sara, and I were in and out of court multiple times. Dawson and I sat on one side of the empty juvenile courtroom, Sara on the other. It was ironic actually; Tom had spent his childhood convinced that he and his mom were victims of the new wife and the uncaring dad, yet here we were, Dawson and I facing Tom—the undeniably guilty party. It had never mattered that we provided the doctors and therapists, the support, and an honest home, while she provided only chaos and neglected him. I did all the mothering things and yet I *wasn't* his mother. It was never about driving him to therapists, teaching him to swim, or endless hours of homework. My advice about friends and girlfriends, consoling him when he was upset about life, it didn't matter. On top of his crimes against the girls, he had actually gone after me personally. I thought he loved me, and it stung to realize not only did he not, but he had used me as the excuse to hurt my babies. I was humbled and angered by this awareness.

I once heard a mother who had lost her kindergarten son in a horrible massacre describe forgiveness as a daily choice to separate herself, disconnect the umbilical cord to the pain that tied her to the murderer. Dressed like I was going to work, stiffly sitting in the corporately designed courtroom, my belly ached, my head spun, and my heart pounded. Everyone in there was a stranger, yet they knew the most intimate details of our life. The only separation between the perpetrator and the victims in those moments were their bodies being in school, not physically present in court. I forced myself to stay numb and maintain hardcore focus on each of the statements passing through the air. Walking into the room last and wrestling a few papers on the dais before he sat down calmly, the judge would open with, "We bring this court to order. . . . Tom, son, are you aware of what the charges against you mean?"

It was surreal. I was in the room and focused, but still somehow disconnected, and that ounce of separation from reality held me together in these moments as if I was watching somebody else's life. My belief that I could teach the girls that the power of their voices potentially saved their brother's life and most definitely saved theirs helped me to endure the process. I was stumped on how to stop the blaming, though. He did it. The psychological reports showed he knew what he was doing. Yes, he was young, but he did it. Nothing could change that: no apology or excuse could restore what had been stolen. After the long days in court, I would drop into bed at night and dream of an eye for an eye or the chance to beat his face to a pulp, but I knew down deep that that wouldn't solve anything. I replayed over and over what I was so often told by probation: "In the end, prepare yourself for everyone to lose."

At the beginning of each court session, Dawson and I entered as a team. We drove to the courthouse making bad jokes about our life, and walked in a bit tense but connected at the pinkies. We usually had a plan if we were expected to talk.

At the end of each court session, the room seemed colder. My face was red with heat. My pinky had no companion. Our bond was weakened. It was the pressure. For lack of any other precedent, the court leaned heavily on my agreement for each step, in spite of the fact that Dawson was the one who did the research and fought to create the next steps for Tom and that all three kids were his. The onus was on the mother of the victims, and, like it or not, that was me. Torn with anguish over the crime and the terrible solution options, I felt suffocated after each session. My throat was often tight, holding back sobs, even though the tears were falling already. I struggled to stand tall with pride but felt exhausted and vulnerable. My body would ever-so-slightly tremble with anxiety releasing itself.

Walking out, I'd see my friend Britt reading her book in the cavernous and vacant hallway outside the courtroom until she heard us. Every step echoed and announced our arrival. Hearing our movements, she would fold up her book, stuff it in her purse, and stand, greeting us both with a smile. She calmed my anger, dried my tears, listened to my venting, took me to lunch, and nurtured whatever emotion had come up with each session. Without judgment Britt just sat patiently and held the weight of my burdens. Her tight hug embraced my crumpled, crying self. She was always kind to Dawson as she took me in the handoff, giving him a hug and an encouraging word before focusing on me. Once in the car, she gave me the floor to roar the day's details and then found in her heart an appropriate amount of equal anger and disdain. Never too much, never too little. Then in her subtle, easy way, she would find a bright side and bring about a laughable moment.

CHAPTER EIGHTEEN

THE CLOSE OF JUNE ALWAYS IGNITED THE SUMMER excitement and freedom from the structure of school days. The girls had also asked for a break from therapy, which I was happy to grant. Our house was now filled with innocent laughter and giggling as doors opened and closed while they ran from one activity to another. With less time in the car, we now just sang loudly at home. We loved our music. Who better to celebrate July thirteenth with than the queen of pop—Taylor Swift (who was notably a thirteen lover herself)? The girl who had laid all her bad out on the music sheets and turned it into gold. But Christmas had come and gone. Taylor's birthday had come and gone. The only way to surprise them was Easter. Yes, that Easter the bunny brought the girls five tickets to the Taylor Swift concert on July thirteenth at MetLife Stadium. We even brought the babysitter. Admittedly, it was a lofty bunny gift. They came downstairs Easter morning and dove right into the jellybeans. More candy and sugar awaited in their colorful plastic eggs. I waited for the moment of truth that lay hidden in one particular egg. Suddenly a noise erupted from the girls that was so loud it startled the dog to her feet. Soon they were giggling and screaming: "Mom, the Easter bunny gave us tickets to Taylor Swift!!!" Conventional parenting had been left behind. That July thirteenth we all danced and sang our hearts out with no cares in the world.

TIME PROVIDED LONGER periods between decisions about Tom, which gave my anxiety longer periods of rest and lessened the conversations around the house, giving the girls a rest from it too. Laughing slowly replaced crying. There was no going back to our old life, but the rhythm of our new "normal" was settling in. This had me reevaluating what I had once thought was important. When I'd met Dawson, I'd told him that I wanted a 1960s convertible Mustang for my fortieth birthday. I envisioned myself driving in it, with the top down, wild and free. It would be my escape from the responsibilities of life, which I had always taken so seriously. Now all I wanted to know was, "What *did* I really want?" I wanted to escape and to get perspective. I wanted freedom and I wanted fresh air. A car didn't solve this, although if I drove long enough, it would take me off the grid. I knew I wanted an experience—a spiritual experience for my spiritual journey. So I approached Dawson about having an adventure in Africa instead of a car. With some quick fishing around, we found someone to help us plan going to Tanzania. By July Dawson had let go of his reservations and committed to this awesome request. His hesitations really only involved how young the girls were, but after the pediatrician strongly advised us to go, we moved into full-force planning for two and a half weeks on the other side of the world. All the stars were aligning perfectly to make the trip happen. Life was opening itself back up, and we were ready to embrace it as our November Thirteenth Party in Tanzania.

IT WAS DAWSON'S one and only Thirteenth Party wish to deliver flowers to thirteen unsuspecting church families in August. So on a wet morning, I was invited down to a friend's house to wade through her rain-soggy gardens and cut as many blooms as I needed. I cut and clipped and protected and packed the back of my car with as many fragrant, colorful flowers as I could. Cold and wet myself, I arrived home and set out to arrange thirteen bouquets for delivery. Then I sat at the kitchen table with a map of our town and marked each delivery spot with an *X*, planning out the most efficient route. The house was quiet, and it was peaceful plotting the tour. Dawson cut his workday short so we could pick up the girls from summer camp to begin delivery. Excited and feeling a bit giddy, we set out to deliver the flowers to thirteen households with our route in hand.

In the days leading up to this, we had worked with the ministry outreach volunteer to create our list, and certainly there were a few families we personally wanted to thank for their kindness to us. I have to admit there was a shyness I felt executing this task. At each house the girls would pick an arrangement, thoughtfully debating from the back of the car. They would skip to the door laughing innocently with Dawson, ring the bell, and watch the surprise and appreciation on the faces of the recipients. With each house they became more confident in their deliveries, and at each house they bounded back to the car in glee. "Mommy, you come to the next door." I was happy to watch from the car, tired from picking, cutting, and arranging. I, instead, enjoyed watching the four hours of delivering from the passenger seat.

৵ৎ

BEFORE LONG, SEPTEMBER and a new school year was upon us. Dawson and I were right back in the principal's office, a place in which I had now spent more time than I'd ever dreamed possible, especially since I had two well-behaved children. Both girls now were in elementary school. And each year, guided by the principal and vice principal, we sat down with the year's new teachers to let them know what had happened. At first it always seemed easy. The principal's office had become comfortable and familiar, the tissues always on her desk and ready. We were all energetic and smiling; everyone exchanged cordial hellos and a few tidbits about their summer. Soon the veil would be lifted and our terrible secret let out. Sure enough, each year the teachers would swallow the lumps in their throats and attempt to keep their surprise and shock inside. Some would cry. Some would bury their heads and write a few notes. Any noise in the room seemed muted. Red faces always replaced slight summer tans. Emotion would overcome me and tears would well and fall. Upon the appearance of my first tears, Dawson would turn red, tilt his head back, and wipe his eyes.

My nose would start to run. Then the tears would grow in size, capturing my voice. Dawson would try turning to control himself. Not because he was mad, but because we were completely vulnerable and exposed in those moments. The principal would break the silence, giving us a moment. Eventually though Dawson would giggle and admit hearing me cry always broke him down. After the initial shock settled, I could give routine information of both girls' mental wellness or signs of distress and then ask if there were any questions.

Usually there were none. The brave ventured to ask about Tom, but our focus was always the girls, and that was sacred in their school.

Energized by new classes, new activities, and new friends, September 2013 was filled with life. Kennedy was in second grade, Taylor in kindergarten. What better way to celebrate a new school year than with cookies? So I set out to have a taste test of thirteen different kinds of cookies.

Unlike the ice cream, I was determined to make each and every kind myself. This required an elaborate plan of time and efficiency for use of the oven. Butter, sugar, and flour decorated the counter. It took two weeks to make every recipe. All the while, at the end of each school day the girls would come home to a sweet-smelling house of freshly baked goods and be tormented when their "Mommy, can we eat one?" was met with "Not yet." The baking kept me from overthinking. I loved considering food combinations instead of PTSD solutions. Old recipes vs. new. Wild ingredients. My mind was laser focused on cookies.

But the day before we were to enjoy them, I realized all my planning had still fallen short. Not every recipe was easy. Some didn't even work. Was this going to be the one month that we fell short? In her own black-and-white, clear way, after hearing my worry, Taylor said, "Mommy, you know that aisle in the grocery store that you always skip? You know, the one with the cookies? Go there—buy some." And on September thirteenth we had salad for dinner and a whole dining table full of cookies to enjoy! Evaluating the sweet aromas; commenting on the crispness or the crunch of each variety; rating the recipes that worked and which we could throw out; loosening our pants to take one more bite and enjoy that last sweet flavor, we were satiated. Taylor was right, sometimes taking the easy way was equally fun.

❧

THAT FALL, INSTEAD of wallowing in our usual season of
discomfort and subconscious memories, we were eagerly preparing for October thirteenth. Throughout August and September, we had hoarded kites of all different kinds, colors,
and sizes as they went on end-of-the-summer sales. Dawson
set up a trip to his sister's in Martha's Vineyard for this endeavor. No one could fly a kite like Uncle Matt, and no place
had a better chance for plenty of wind than an island. I had
mixed memories of our previous time on Martha's Vineyard,
so I approached it yet again with my own heaviness and hesitation.

Like clockwork, after the car doors shut for the drive to
the ferry, my knees went toward the passenger-side door and
my chin began to quiver. I turned my head sideways just as
we got on the highway. Here I went again: eyes welling up
and tears ready to roll. Another wave of grief spilling out of
me. Grieving had become a long and endless process for me
and I was still easily triggered, by memories that were now
rewritten.

I felt relief, however, when we finally arrived at Woods
Hole. Tahoe and I stayed in the car; I was happy for the quiet. Dawson and the girls went up to the top of the boat for
fresh air, leaving the large garage beneath the boat that was
now filled with cars.

When we finally landed on Martha's Vineyard, it was
late, so quick hellos led to quick good nights.

In the morning we tested out a few kites to get warmed
up. Uncle Matt acted as our meteorologist and reported that
the winds would be better the next day. Dawson and I had

been coming to their island house all nine of our years together. I thought we had explored the island entirely, but I
was wrong. The island still had some surprises.

We were four adults, two kids, and two dogs with packed
coolers, a pile of towels, and bottles of sunscreen stuffed into
two island cars. We took the road less traveled to South
Beach, a usual spot for us. Matt let the air out of the tires
and drove us through the dunes and past the crowds, down
the beach where the grass thinned. At the end of the point,
we were completely surrounded by space, time, and water.
The sound of waves crashing on the shore was now accompanied by the sound of two rambunctious kids and two very
playful puppies. We lazed the day away reading, swimming,
and building sand castles. The newness of the situation allowed me to relax and finally just breathe. When our skin
was chafed by the sand and dry from the sun, we packed up
the cars and headed out. Just a quick stop at the house to
drop the coolers, and we were off again to the other side of
the island for a hike. My shell of defenses was softening, and
slowly I felt lovable again.

Exhausted from the day, we ate a quick dinner and got
right to sleep. Relaxed and filled with new memories, I felt
ready.

Since this was one of the first thirteen ideas and we'd
waited until October to execute it, we had high hopes. We
packed up fifteen kites just in case one or two broke or didn't
fly, and we headed out to Edgartown lighthouse. Matt had
scouted locations before our arrival on the island and
thought the grassy area made for great places to station each
kite. The first few went up low and easy. As we widened our
flying space, people passing by would ask, "What are you

doing?" One of us would explain that we were attempting to fly thirteen kites at the same time. After an inquisitive look, we would often get asked *why*—to which the only responses were, "Our daughters wanted to," or "Why not?"

The bigger kites needed more wind and more patience; numbers nine and ten were proving to be frustrating. Even Kennedy, my forever optimist, was getting impatient with her repeated effort. One of the bigger kites just wouldn't fly. After getting up, it took an immediate nosedive back into the sand. We had already broken one kite. Although it was a relatively small thing, it was hard to watch her hopes dashed over this. I needed to control this moment, even if it was just a kite. With determination and a pep talk, we regrouped and began chanting, "We can do it!" over and over, louder and louder. With nothing more than innocence and hope, we got that kite in the air.

Now with twelve of the kites flying nicely, number thirteen—Uncle Matt's old faithful—sprung a tear. We had a moment of panic. The spectacle of our turmoil—two barking dogs running loose and two small blond girls holding kites on a wide-open beach with eight other kites buried with anchors—turned spectators, tourists, and vacationers heads with wonder. Additionally two adults were also toting kites in hand. All of us were cheering each other on with encouraging words, while Uncle Matt was jerry-rigging the last kite to get it into the air. Off in a far corner of the beach, I was waiting for the final flight in a desperate attempt to actually get it all on camera.

At the precise moment Matt got number thirteen up, I snapped shots wildly, thinking I had gotten the proof of our escapade. Within ten minutes our egos were soaring, even if our kites were no longer. Satisfied that we had accomplished the impossible, we now had six hungry stomachs, so we dropped the kites easily and abruptly ended our endeavor.

ℒ CHAPTER NINETEEN

ONCE OCTOBER WAS COMPLETED, THE RACE WAS ON FOR the big trip. We were ready to move beyond anticipation and into our African adventure. It was a matter of days now until we left.

Carefully sorted piles of medicines, clothes, travel food, and provisions were sprawled across the floor waiting to be packed. Immunizations were done and passports ready. We had gotten school permission from the superintendent and the principal. Our inner circle and family, doctors, therapists, and teachers happily cheered on our adventure idea from the sidelines.

TRUTHFULLY, WE HAD no idea what we were doing. Tanzania was a world away and our knowledge was from textbooks and news stories. Nothing can prepare you for the world of wonder that we were about to enter.

An eight-hour plane ride to Amsterdam, or as a fatigued Taylor called it, Hamster Dam, and nine more to Tanzania kicked off the seventeen-day excursion.

We arrived to our first destination on a private land reservation at the base of Mount Kilimanjaro in the middle of the night. Exhausted, we saw nothing but darkness and went straight to sleep in our new and foreign environment.

Thousands of miles away from our tragic life back home, the next morning we rose to vast landscape and clear blue skies that went on forever, making even the mountains look small. Our eyes soaked in the totally new colors. We saw every shade of brown and tan in the bushes and grass and then there were little pops of purple mixed in. Elephants and giraffes meandered around us like neighborhood street cats. Masses of baboons blocked the roads and cleaned each other without a care in the world that we were staring at them. Completely surrounded by newness, every sound and sight was of interest. That morning, our adventure became real, leaving us speechless and filled with a million questions.

Oxygen inflated our lungs. I didn't have time for any of the routine thoughts of my life back home, no need to look at my watch and get ready to feed someone or get them off to an activity. New thoughts swirled in our heads. "Mommy, what kind of animal is that?" "Look, Mom!" "Dad, do you see that bird?" "Mom, Mom, Mom . . ." For the next two and a half weeks, we spent ten-hour days exploring and traveled from country to city and back to the country. At the end of each day, the girls vigorously wrote in their journals about all their experiences, like seeing a black rhino and waiting for the cheetah cub who had jumped up on the hood of our Jeep. Everything was something to report and remember. The lion kill, the baboon jumping on Kennedy's head, the children they played with from the orphanage. The herds of zebra and wildebeest . . . We tried to chronicle it all.

☙

A FEW DAYS into the trip was Kennedy's seventh birthday, and also the day Dawson and I had planned to renew our vows. Dawson had met the priest with whom he'd been communicating before our arrival. In the confusion of their overseas conversations, the priest had assumed he was marrying us for the first time. Since we had left behind the people we once were, the priest's homily resonated as if it *was*, in fact, a first-time marriage. "No two human beings are made for each other. Every human being is made for God. Marriages are not made in heaven. There are no prefabricated marriages. They are made here on earth, day by day. . . . Your love of God and your love for one another must overflow to others. In marriage we leave our father and mother. Your own family now becomes your first priority . . . and you should have a special love for those who come to you in need." As he spoke, my tears flowed freely; then every time I looked at Dawson he giggled at his own teary eyes, shrugging like he couldn't help himself but to cry and laugh. "The family is the society we belong to. We are born into a family not into a church. . . . The purpose of the family is to raise human beings. And the function of the Christian family is to raise Christian human beings. . . . We have to make the family work. There is no substitute for it."

Just as we completed our vows, the largest rainbow I have ever seen colored the sky and a light shower began to fall. As the rain started, the orphanage children began to sing and celebrate the water and our union. Slowly the rainbow grew wider and longer from left to right, filling the sky. To me it was a message. Then a second rainbow appeared. Yes, an undeniable message from God, like that to Noah. Good things will come.

I hungered to feel this liberty and relaxation forever. I no longer felt defeat. I was alive.

FOR THE REST of the trip, I let myself stop feeling like the prisoner I believed myself to be at home. My head was now filled with awe and wonder about the beauty in untouched nature, the love and generosity of the people who had so little, and hope. Hate was peeled away from my inner core, revealing passion I never knew I had.

I never quite looked at things the same way once we came home from Africa. Reentry was difficult. As Americans I felt like we had an abundance of everything. I looked around town and everyone had electricity, clean water, clothes, schools, expensive cars, perfectly manicured lawns. We had everything! At a routine dentist appointment, the doctor asked Kennedy and Taylor what they wanted for Christmas, and at the same time they both answered, "Nothing." He looked at me and said, "What did you do to them?" To which I replied that we had just returned from Tanzania. Having done lots of service work himself, he nodded and said, "I see." But then he knelt down to eye level with the girls and said, "You have been given a great gift."

We were arrested by an awakening of generosity. We wanted to help hurting people rather than *being* hurt people.

December was already upon us when we returned, and our final thirteenth idea came to us at church on a Sunday morning. The minister did the usual final call for volunteers to fill the Dove program food boxes for the needy. This box was meant to fill a pantry and give Christmas dinner to those who could otherwise not afford it. It was more fun to give to a whole family, so the singles were often left till the end. There were thirteen left to be filled, actually. As always, I found it to be a sign; so did the girls, as they quickly leaned in to me and whispered, "Mom, we have to . . ." They didn't even complete the sentence, but I knew what they were thinking. When church ended, I subtly rushed out and snatched up every last one. While I was bent over the table filling out the cards to assume responsibility for each meal, another parishioner asked me what I was doing. I said that we would fill the last thirteen. She looked rather perplexed but let me continue on. By now most of our friends and social circle had heard of our year of thirteens.

Each meal had a list of about thirty pantry items that needed to be added to the box for completion. They ranged from smaller-size boxes, like tea, to heavier containers, like peanut butter and Parmalat. I envisioned myself in the grocery store with two grocery carts filled to the brim with nearly four hundred items and decided to take advantage of Peapod, the delivery service for food in our area, instead. Four hundred dollars and lots of bags later, all the food was delivered to our door. Food covered the kitchen table and all six chairs, the dining room table, and every one of its chairs. Pantry items were sprawled everywhere.

Each Dove box, as they were called, had to be packed in two boxes for the person receiving it. This meant that on top of purchasing all the food, we needed to assemble the twenty-six shipping boxes. We created our own assembly line. I called out the product, and the girls found it and filled a box, checking it off the list as we went. Hours passed with few words other than our list items . . . jelly, cookies, crackers, soup, beans. Little by little, our table space was freed up and the boxes were filled. Eventually we made space on the open kitchen table for Dawson to wrap the supper-sized gifts. By the time we were done, all that was left of a Costco-sized roll of holiday paper was the scraps and cuttings from the wrapping of the boxes and a wall of well-organized Christmas treasures for thirteen individuals.

All smiles, mission accomplished. We had celebrated as a family on the thirteenth of every month and our 2013, a year of healing, was complete.

✺ CHAPTER TWENTY

September 2014

"I stand before the court today to deliver an impact statement preceding the pronouncement of the final verdict against Tom. When Dawson and I were asked by the court to speak on behalf of ourselves and our girls, I was daunted by the request. Stressed and feeling a huge sense of responsibility, I asked myself, where do I even begin to describe the influence this series of events has had and will continue to have on our lives? How can I possibly sum it up? How do we find freedom from this permanent loss of innocence or measure the death of a trusted relationship? How can I express to you, merely bystanders, what it felt like to be in this head-on collision—wrecked; body parts strewn everywhere; Dawson legless; me armless; helpless to put the truly wounded victims, Kennedy and Taylor, back together in a way that was recognizable; doctors and hospitals too far removed to help with the triage; and all around us powerless onlookers demanding we hurry up and fix all of this damage. *I can't. I can't sum it up.* And yet, for you to understand the bottomless depths of my family's despair as a result of Tom's actions, I will have to try.

Tom blew up our world. There isn't a day that goes by that we are not confronted by the consequences of his actions. Kennedy and Taylor have nightmares and crippling flashbacks. They are understandably angry and carry guilty feelings for a crime they did not commit. They have developed countless fears: of monsters, transitions, holding on, letting go; of boys in general but of teenage boys specifically. Their anxiety manifests in ways that are unexpected—sometimes they bite their nails until they are bloody, or in the throes of fear will lose control and urinate on themselves in public. Anywhere can be a trigger—the school lunch line, our pool club, a playdate, a plate of once-loved foods on the dining room table. They struggle with their own sexuality; feelings that would be normal for someone else and appropriate for their age make them feel uncomfortable or act out. They will never get to be innocent young girls. Their virginity is lost; and only now are they developing their understanding of this. They will never get to fully escape from the memory of what was done to them, and they may grapple forever in big and small ways with the horror of their pasts.

Beyond our immediate family, Tom has negatively affected everyone within his circle of influence, from our large extended families to our friends, right on down to the babysitters that were burdened by knowing his terrible secret.

In order to survive the irreparable damage Tom has done, we will forever remain a family of four and not five. We cannot coexist together ever again. We are working as a unit and as individuals to figure out what it means to navigate through this trying time in our lives. If this had happened to someone else, I never could have grasped how lonely and devastating, how terrifying it would be to journey into this dark and uncharted territory together. We lean heavily on our faith as a means of support, sure in the knowledge that we could not fix this mess alone. We will, however, rise above the carnage because we must. We were broken and we are changed, but we love each other and we are unafraid of the future. We walk toward it hand in hand.

Tom's impact was immeasurable. But it will not define us. Love has the final say."

๏ EPILOGUE

WHEN MY LIFE WAS UPENDED THAT TERRIBLE NIGHT IN October 2011, I wasn't a person who had ever known how to quit. I soon discovered my energy was finite, however. I had to go on but I had no roadmap as to how to do that; and neither did anyone else. My lack of understanding sent me searching for answers. I just looked up and kept looking up because looking down felt like giving in. The sky, the wind, the trees, the universe—that is where I found God, wisdom, and strength. It's not in any mother's dreams to nurse her children from being victims into survivorship. I simply could not have imagined it would happen, let alone to me.

More than anything I still wanted what every mom wanted. I wanted my kids to be kind and ready to receive love with open hearts. I wanted them to be innocent and free to be kids even though they had been thrust into maturity way too soon. I could not take for granted that any of those things would "just come" though. I had to make the way. I was never alone, but I still felt incredible loneliness.

"Your family is so close. I can tell you all have a special bond." Friends have observed and told me this repeatedly over the years. Though nobody had ever asked me directly about the specifics, most people who knew us realized that something had gone wrong and respected our privacy. The parents of the girls' peers, Kennedy's crowd at least, knew about Tom once upon a time. Taylor's may or may not have ever even known he existed. People in general accepted his absence.

It made sense really; there were no pictures of him at our house, no vacation visits from private school. No crayon drawings on the refrigerator of a family of five. After he left, his room was disassembled, his possessions given away or thrown out. He disappeared overnight. We didn't talk about him in public. He didn't have any achievements we shared with our friends. We weren't proud of any athletic awards he had won. He was just gone.

Our trauma was fast and furious. At the time, people repeatedly told us that time healed all wounds. I wanted to punch those people. I hated hearing that time was "on my side." Yet it's true; time takes me further away from the triggers and the horrifying memories. Time gives me space to get my bearings and trust my own instincts again. Time gives me healing and replaces chaos with peace.

I have never been a "people person." I am certainly not lovey-dovey; yet today when people see Dawson and me together, I am often complimented on how "cute we are" and even accused of exuding love. I still can't answer to my girls why Tom did what he did. Maybe I never will. But I did receive gifts of great love in my marriage, in my children, and in my faith. Some things, like grace and forgiveness and "unburied" saints, simply remain mysteries.

Our photo album includes some pretty unflattering pictures. But we are united because we looked closely at every ugly image and owned that those too were ours. We are who we are because we walked through it with an army of angels helping us get to the other side.

I love you Dawson, Kennedy, and Taylor. You are my saints.

ABOUT THE AUTHOR

BRIN MILLER grew up in an affluent suburb outside of New York City. A graduate of Denison University, she was an all-American swimmer who married her childhood sweetheart and climbed the corporate ladder with the same drive and determination that had served her well growing up. After her first marriage failed, she remarried in 2004. In her early thirties, she had everything a modern American woman was supposed to want—but behind closed doors, her family grappled with betrayal, anger, and blame. In an attempt to pull back the curtain on a world many consider "secret and untouchable," Miller has chronicled her harrowing experience of bringing her children back from the trauma of sexual abuse at the hand of a close relative.

SELECTED TITLES FROM SHE WRITES PRESS

She Writes Press is an independent publishing company
founded to serve women writers everywhere.
Visit us at www.shewritespress.com.

Off the Rails: One Family's Journey Through Teen Addiction by Susan
Burrowes. $16.95, 978-1-63152-467-7. An inspiring story of family
love, determination, and the last-resort intervention that helped
one troubled young woman find sobriety after a terrifying and
harrowing journey.

Searching for Normal: The Story of a Girl Gone Too Soon by Karen
Meadows. $16.95, 978-1-63152-137-9. Karen Meadows inter-
twines her own story with excerpts from her daughter Sadie's
journals to describes their roller coaster ride through Sadie's depression and a maze of inadequate mental health treatment and
services—one that ended with Sadie's suicide at age eighteen.

*Blinded by Hope: One Mother's Journey Through Her Son's Bipolar Illness
and Addiction* by Meg McGuire. $16.95, 978-1-63152-125-6. A
fiercely candid memoir about one mother's roller coaster ride
through doubt and denial as she attempts to save her son from
substance abuse and bipolar illness.

Raising Myself: A Memoir of Neglect, Shame, and Growing Up Too Soon
by Beverly Engel. $16.95, 978-1-63152-367-0. A powerfully in-
spiring and unflinchingly honest story of how best-selling author
and abuse recovery expert Beverly Engel made her way in the
world—in spite of her mother's neglect and constant criticism,
undergoing sexual abuse at nine, and being raped at twelve.

Say It Out Loud: Revealing and Healing the Scars of Sexual Abuse by
Roberta Dolan. $16.95, 978-1-938314-99-5. An in-depth guide to
healing the wounds caused by sexual abuse, written by a survivor
who's lived the process firsthand.

Secrets in Big Sky Country: A Memoir by Mandy Smith. $16.95,
978-1-63152-814-9. A bold and unvarnished memoir about the
shattering consequences of familial sexual abuse—and the
strength it takes to overcome them.